DOUBLE-DIGIT GROWTH

DOUBLE-DIGIT
GROWTH

How Great Companies Achieve It—

No Matter What

MICHAEL TREACY

PORTFOLIO

PORTFOLIO
Published by the Penguin Group
Penguin Group (USA) Inc., 375 Hudson Street, New York, New York 10014, U.S.A.
Penguin Books Ltd, 80 Strand, London WC2R 0RL, England
Penguin Books Australia Ltd, 250 Camberwell Road, Camberwell,
    Victoria 3124, Australia
Penguin Books Canada Ltd, 10 Alcorn Avenue,
    Toronto, Ontario, Canada M4V 3B2
Penguin Books India (P) Ltd, 11 Community Centre, Panchsheel Park,
    New Delhi – 110 017, India
Penguin Books (N.Z.) Ltd, Cnr Rosedale and Airborne Roads, Albany,
    Auckland, New Zealand
Penguin Books (South Africa) (Pty) Ltd, 24 Sturdee Avenue,
    Rosebank, Johannesburg 2196, South Africa

Penguin Books Ltd, Registered Offices:
80 Strand, London WC2R 0RL, England

First published in 2003 by Portfolio,
a member of Penguin Group (USA) Inc.

10   9   8   7   6   5   4   3   2   1

PUBLISHER'S NOTE
This publication is designed to provide accurate and authoritative information in regard to
the subject matter covered. It is sold with the understanding that the publisher is not engaged
in rendering legal, accounting or other professional services. If you require legal advice or
other expert assistance, you should seek the services of a competent professional.

LIBRARY OF CONGRESS CATALOGING-IN-PUBLICATION DATA

Treacy, Michael.
    Double-digit growth : how great companies achieve it, no matter what / by Michael Treacy.
        p. cm.
    Includes index.
    ISBN 1-59184-005-8
        1. Corporations—United States—Growth—Management.   2. Strategic planning.
    3. Management—United States.   I. Title.

    HD2785.T74 2003
    658.4'06—dc21   2003050678

This book is printed on acid-free paper. ∞

Printed in the United States of America
Set in Adobe Garamond with Optima

Beautiful Evelyn
So giving of life and love—
My only desire

Acknowledgments

The central thesis of this book—that any business can achieve steady double-digit growth—isn't for everyone. After all, there isn't enough growth in our economy for *every* company to achieve double-digit growth. But *your* organization can achieve it, even if others can't. If you believe this, or want to believe this, then this book is written for you.

When I began gathering data for *Double-Digit Growth* more than five years ago, my hypothesis was that the difference between steady fast-growth businesses and also-rans would be found in their strategy. Growth companies must be making different decisions, placing different bets, and building better strategies than everyone else, I thought. As the research progressed, however, and more data were gathered and analyzed, what became clear was that the major difference was that high-growth firms approached the challenge of growth in a more sophisticated way. They built robust portfolios of growth initiatives that spread risk and improved the predictability of results. Further, they employed sophisticated management systems for planning, controlling, and measuring growth that were different from other organizations in the study. In slower or unsteady growth firms, growth management was a much more haphazard process.

Steady double-digit growth was the result of a comprehensive system for managing growth as a portfolio of opportunities and initiatives. Any firm can adopt this system for managing a growth portfolio and achieve steady double-digit growth. This book describes how.

Over the years, I have had the good fortune to know scores of executives who have generously hosted me at their companies for discussion, debate, and discourse about the challenges and opportunities they wrestle with on a daily basis. Some of those conversations stand out as seminal learning opportunities, including those with Keith Bailey, Marc Belton, Scott Bush, Michael Dell, Mike Eskew, J. P. Garnier, Michael Glenn, Joe Grano, Clay Jones, Jerry Karabelas, Bob Kistinger, John Leggate, Steve Maritz, Frank McKone, Joe Nacchio, Jim Orr, Howard Pien, Ron Sargent, Rick Scott, Naomi Seligman, Bill Stavropoulos, Tom Stemberg, David Stern, Jim Swartz, Bob Tobin, and Laurie Tucker. From each of these people I took away something that found its way into this book.

Three executives with whom I have worked deserve special mention. Charlie Fote has been generous with his time and allowed me to study his company, First Data Corporation, in great detail. Charlie is a complete executive—strategically insightful, operationally engaged, unfailingly inspirational, and boundlessly energetic. I stand in awe of his capacities.

John Weber ranks among the very best executives whom I have met. He has a remarkable ability to reduce growth and profit issues to their simplest and clearest terms and motivate a management team to exceed his high expectations for performance.

It has been almost ten years since I last worked with Gerry Schwartz of Onex Corporation, but I've not forgotten the lessons I learned observing a world-class investor in action. Gerry continues to guide his firm to ever greater heights.

I have had the very good fortune to spend long hours discussing all manner of growth and governance issues with several colleagues while this book was in development. Disque Deane is a good friend who has had a long and distinguished career as a Wall Street investment banker. He has been generous with his experience and insights about acquisitions and investing. David Roberts and Ian Foottit are consulting colleagues with whom I have worked extensively and from whom I have gained much insight.

The further from MIT's Sloan School that I travel, the more clearly I understand the profound effect that my ten years there has had on me. In particular, I owe a debt of gratitude to Jack Rockart, Tom Magnanti, and John Henderson, who each affected my thinking in very different ways.

Many organizations have been generous in sharing their data with me, including two companies that carefully track the automotive industry. Tom Libby and Melissa Church of J. D. Power and Associates provided market-share information and Mellisa Mullen of R. L. Polk provided customer-retention data that were invaluable in my analyses. Thanks also to Todd Krieger of John Bailey and Associates for his help in securing some of these data.

My business partner, Jim Sims, has afforded me the time to focus on this book project. He is a good friend, a generous business partner, a great deal maker, and an uncommonly decent human being. Thanks also to Nicole Ames and Shawn DeLorey for helping to make this book a success.

In large part this book came about because Helen Rees, my literary agent, gently pushed me for many years to write another book. Helen is a loyal and dedicated advisor. When the mud's flying, trust me, you want this woman in your corner.

Two individuals were invaluable in the process of making this book a reality: Donna Sammons Carpenter, a veritable word goddess, and Maurice Coyle, a master of structure and story. Thanks also to the team at Wordworks: Larry Martz, Toni Porcelli, Cindy Sammons, Robert Shnayerson, and Robert Stock. Without their editorial support, this book wouldn't be half as much fun to read.

My publisher at Penguin's Portfolio, Adrian Zackheim, has displayed unwavering enthusiasm for this book and patience with me, even as I missed not one but three deadlines. Thank you, Adrian. And to Will Weisser, Portfolio's marketing director, thank you for what is to come.

A final thank you goes to Evelyn, Parker, Hunter, and Tegan. Your support and love mean everything to me.

Needham, Massachusetts
April 2003

Contents

DOUBLE-DIGIT GROWTH

1

Why Is It So Hard to Grow?

- Which has grown faster since 1997: Intel or inflation? If you picked Intel, you lose.
- After spending $100 billion on acquisitions over five years, AT&T's CEO Michael Armstrong achieved (a) higher revenues, (b) no gain, or (c) lower revenues. Incredibly, the answer is (c).
- In 1997, Procter & Gamble's CEO vowed to double its business in seven years. If it continues to grow at the pace that it has actually set since then, how many more years will it take to reach its goal: two, twelve, or twenty-five? Answer: yes, twenty-five years. P&G is a little behind schedule because it's only managed to grow an average of 2.4 percent annually since 1997.
- What does Revlon blame its growth woes on: a weak economy, political uncertainties, or competition? Answer: all three. Management apparently believes that mascara sales are very sensitive to political uncertainties.
- In 2000, Gateway Computer declared in its annual report that pursuing growth would be "kind of silly" that year. Could Gateway do anything sillier? Yes. The company skipped growth in 2001 and 2002 as well, so its revenues shrank for all three years.
- When Chris Galvin became Motorola's chief executive in 1997, the company earned more than $1 billion a year. By how much have

the corporation's profits since exceeded Galvin's compensation? Answer: by zero. While Galvin took home $45 million, Motorola reported a cumulative loss. Worse, Galvin messed up revenues as well.

• IBM's much-touted CEO, Lou Gerstner, grew the company's business-service revenues at double-digit rates. True or false? False. Big Blue's service revenues actually rose a mere 5 percent in 2001, Gerstner's last year at the helm, and only 3 percent the year before (so much for the myth that IBM owns the service business). During Gerstner's entire ten-year reign, in fact, mighty IBM's overall growth averaged 2.9 percent a year, barely enough to stay ahead of inflation.

• Is Caterpillar now the world's number-two or number-three maker of farm equipment? Trick question. In 2001, the big Cat sold its agricultural division for a loss, after getting plowed under by John Deere. It's now limping along with 2 percent annual revenue growth, flat gross profits, and declining earnings.

• "We're convinced, in fact, that the greatest challenge ahead may be simply keeping up with the demand." Which eminent CEO spoke those brave words eighteen months before his company's revenues plummeted by $6 billion? None other than Scott McNealy of Sun Microsystems.

I could go on and on. In fact, I could rip down the entire list of *Fortune* 500 companies, or the *Fortune* Global 500 for that matter, and redline case after case of supposedly healthy businesses in a comatose state of feeble growth, no growth, or actual shrinkage. And don't blame it all on today's floundering economy. Throughout the heady nineties, these major companies hardly grew at all. While others boomed, they straggled along in slow motion, sometimes not going bust thanks only to creative accounting.

What's going on? The truth is that big chunks of Corporate America, along with their counterparts in Asia and Europe, have fallen victim to no-growth paralysis—a broad, profound, systemic illness worsened by constant denial. It represents a serious threat to the health of the business community here and around the world.

Growth is the oxygen of business, the key to business life or death. Growing enterprises thrive; shrinking companies vanish. Why, then, is a lack of growth the dirty little secret of today's corporations? Why are so many companies, in fact, blocked, stalled, or stunted? Why do so many managers preside over no-growth organizations without confronting the reality that accepting the status quo is the business equivalent of committing suicide?

This book offers my answer. It argues that the way we think about and pursue business growth is fundamentally flawed and overdue for a dramatically new approach. To that end, I have identified a portfolio of five growth disciplines that, followed with care and dedication, can aid any enterprise—yours included—in achieving steady, double-digit growth year after year. In the chapters to come, I describe and analyze each of these disciplines along with specific insights and strategies to help in their application. Throughout, I show how companies of every size and variety have learned to mix and match the disciplines in the portfolio to fit their individual needs. The goal: to provide a simple, practical guide to point your company toward substantial, sustainable growth.

My work as a consultant over the past eight years has focused exclusively on the challenge of growth. It has taken me to corporations large and small, some growing spectacularly, others in decline. In most cases, I found that senior management was poorly equipped to meet the challenges of growth.

But I also found organizations that achieved double-digit growth year after year. Such value-multipliers included well-known stars—among them Wal-Mart, Harley Davidson, Starbucks, and Dell. These major winners shared an intense focus on customer value that I described in my book, *The Discipline of Market Leaders*. But as I continued to follow their success over the years, I realized that their dramatic growth derived from something beyond their customer focus, crucial as that was. The secret was not a single magic bullet; it was their ability to combine many skills and strengths in a sustained, relentless way that made each company a powerhouse, virtually unbeatable in its field.

I soon observed that other companies—including H&R Block, Lowe's, Johnson Controls, and Medtronic—were achieving double-digit growth with less publicity but equally impressive results that could not be attributed to any single cause, such as brilliant positioning, a powerhouse product, or sheer luck. It became increasingly clear that winners prevailed not because they grew in sudden spurts but rather because they grew in steady strides. These companies managed growth in effective ways that delivered sustainable, predictable results.

Even more intriguing was my discovery that a large number of virtually anonymous organizations—such as Mohawk Industries, Paychex, Oshkosh Truck, Manitowoc, and Biomet—have also been achieving double-digit gains in revenue, gross profits, and net income over many years. If they can do it, I began to ask myself, why can't Intel, AT&T, Procter & Gamble, Revlon, Motorola, IBM, Caterpillar, and Sun?

The amazing disparity between so many stalled companies with famous logos and so many relatively obscure steady-growers was a phenomenon I had to investigate further. It led me to formally study the growth habits of some 130 businesses of all kinds and sizes. The insights gained from this research comprise the heart of my argument for a drastic improvement in the management systems, tools, and techniques by which corporations achieve growth.

Right now, growth management in many organizations is almost laughable. Ask nearly any management team to meet a cost budget, cut 10 percent from its expenses, or implement a new process improvement, and it is generally up to the task. That's because the techniques for achieving these results are well understood. But ask the same managers to grow at double-digit rates, and they typically look blank. They clearly lack the tools—the disciplines—to tackle growth in a structured, systematic way.

Here's a simple test of whether your management team is equipped to handle growth. It measures whether it has the baseline information needed to make sense out of your company's past growth. Can your team answer these questions?

• How much growth did customer churn cost your business last year? If your company had retained its customer base as successfully as the best competitor in your industry, how much faster would your business have grown?

• How much of your company's gain in market share was achieved by selling more to its current customers, as opposed to attracting new customers from competitors?

• Has it been cheaper in your industry to grow market share organically or to acquire competitors?

• If your organization had been positioned only in the fastest-growing segments of your market, how much faster would it have grown?

• What have been the three fastest-growing markets adjacent to your market, where the company's key capabilities could have been leveraged for advantage? How much growth did your enterprise achieve in each of them?

• How much of your corporation's growth is attributable to new markets that it entered in the past five years?

If you can answer these questions, your company probably has a disciplined approach to managing growth. If you can't, you don't.

Too many management teams view double-digit growth as something beyond their control—a sudden change in customer taste, say, or an unexpected breakthrough in the research labs. They assume it's all in the lap of the gods, like winning the lottery. They have no idea that it is the result of disciplined management practices.

The growth stagnation this book diagnoses and treats is hardly confined to marginal organizations. For many businesses, single-digit growth has become the norm. Why do so many managers accept low growth? Is it because they secretly love the status quo and are afraid of change? *Growth,* after all, rivals *profit* as the most sacred word in the business canon. No, this contagion of dither and drift—of sheer standing still—is more likely caused by ignorance than by fear. Growth ignorance has seemingly numbed good business minds and dumbed down managerial response.

The result is startling: from 1997 to 2002, the thirty corporations that make up the prestigious Dow Jones Average grew at a collective annual rate of only 4.9 percent in revenues, 4 percent in gross profits, and 0.5 percent in after-tax profits. And those numbers, bad as they are, are tilted by such strong performers as Home Depot, Merck, Microsoft, Wal-Mart, and CitiGroup. Exclude them, and you see that after-tax profits of the remaining twenty-five companies have actually shrunk since 1997, while revenues and gross profits have grown at 2.3 percent and 1.6 percent a year, respectively, about the rate of inflation.

The conclusion is inescapable: a growth disease is debilitating scores of corporations, sapping their vigor and vision, to say nothing of their life expectancy. To better understand the disease, let's examine its pernicious effect on just one organization, Corning, once a healthy giant of the fiber-optics industry, now an invalid with a tenuous chance of recovery.

Virtuous Cycles Become Vicious Cycles

In 2000, Corning's annual report brimmed with good cheer: "Looking forward to 2001, Corning will continue to invest in new-product development, capacity expansion, and external growth. Corning expects its sales will grow by 20 percent to 25 percent and that each segment's net income will show double-digit growth."

Corning managers had some reason to be optimistic. After all, they had just closed the books on their second year of double-digit growth. After bouncing around between $3 billion and $4 billion of revenues since 1990, Corning had really taken off in 1999, booking a 24 percent increase in sales. The following year was even better. Revenues reached $7.1 billion, a 50 percent increase in a single year. It was only natural for Corning's management to focus on those two years, when the telecommunications bubble greatly expanded demand for fiber cable, rather than on the previous nine years, when the same management team had failed to achieve consistent growth.

Corning's predictions about growth turned out to be double delusions. The spring of 2001, just when the 2000 annual report was issued, was Corning's last heyday. In the afterglow of its 2000 performance, the company launched a celebration called "150 Years of Innovation" and happily found itself on now-defunct *Red Herring*'s list of the one hundred most innovative businesses. Unhappily, the heyday soured fast. Corning shares plunged tenfold from the fall of 2000 to that spring of 2001. Unlike thousands of small investors, Wall Street professionals quickly discounted Corning's golden immediate past. They perceived a leaden future—the steady collapse of top Corning customers in telecommunications and electronics, a debacle that astute investors surmised would inevitably ravage Corning itself. They dumped the company's shares by the millions, driving its market value through the floor.

When the books closed on the year 2001, Wall Street's evaluation was proven accurate. Corning reported a decline in revenues of 12 percent, spread across every division, and a huge operating loss of $5.5 billion. Wall Street buzzed with rumors about an impending bankruptcy. The following year proved to be even worse. Revenues declined a further 50 percent to $3.2 billion, and the company reported additional losses of $1.4 billion. In a mere two years, the corporation wiped out two decades of earnings; revenues returned to their 1990 level.

What happened to Corning? Simple: its managers' growth strategy failed completely. Instead of double-digit sales growth, it produced double-digit declines. Lifted to historic highs by a tidal wave of demand, the stock plummeted when the demand suddenly receded, leaving the company as helpless as a beached whale. Quite simply, Corning managers were seduced by a demand bubble they thought would never end. They were unable to use their good fortunes to build an effective approach to growth, which had been so glaringly absent before the bubble. They failed to see that growth endures not because of fortuitous demand, a hot product, or any single tactic. Growth endures when management follows a portfolio of disciplines to ensure that a broad set of growth opportunities are identified and captured as routinely as costs are controlled and processes improved. The Corning mess is a cautionary tale for all businesses, especially those given to taking growth for granted.

Companies decay when they stop growing. That's because growth is a self-reinforcing process that builds on past performance. It is driven by three virtuous cycles that act as catalysts, ensuring that the more you grow, the easier it is to grow even more. Conversely, the less you grow, the harder it is to grow at all—the vicious cycle.

During Corning's two heady growth years, its managers benefited from these virtuous cycles. Little did they anticipate the destructive force unleashed when virtuous cycles reverse direction and become destructive.

The first virtuous cycle is economic. Faster growth leads to higher price/earnings (P/E) multiples, which, in turn, lead to a higher share price, since shareholders can anticipate higher future earnings. Higher share prices enable a company to raise capital more cheaply, whether it borrows money or issues new shares. More capital makes possible more investment, which, in turn, drives higher growth.

When growth slowed at Corning, its P/E multiple and share price dropped precipitously. Capital became more expensive and more difficult to raise. Result: having recently spent more than $10 billion on growth-oriented acquisitions, Corning was forced to raise cash by selling a valued division to 3M for a relatively cheap $840 million. The corporation next slashed capital spending and severely cut research and development. Having sacrificed long-term investment for short-term survival, Corning has made it difficult to reignite growth in the future.

The second virtuous cycle of growth is about momentum. Fast growth gets the attention of customers, both current and potential; it also boosts customer confidence and enhances a company's reputation for excellence. Customer confidence drives higher growth rates. It's that simple: customers want to do business with winners.

Corning's troubles had the opposite effect. With each announcement graver than the last, Corning's best customers were forced to insulate themselves from these problems. How? They sought out additional sources of supply, reducing their dependence on Corning, and demanded that Corning give them better contractual terms—moves that inevitably impeded Corning's efforts to restart growth.

The third virtuous growth cycle is about opportunity. Growth leads to new job opportunities within the organization, which, in turn, lead to higher morale. High morale makes it easier to achieve innovations and improve productivity, the fuel of better customer value. A better value proposition drives faster growth.

Faced with falling revenues, Corning managers knew they had to reduce costs. Choosing a necessary but destructive option, they froze salaries, eliminated twelve thousand jobs, and permanently shuttered half a dozen plants in 2001. Morale was shattered, thus launching another vicious cycle. Innovation and productivity suffered, depressing the value proposition. Shattered dreams were heaped on dead ambitions. Morale and opportunity hit bottom.

Much to their dismay, Corning managers discovered early in 2002 that they had not done enough. It was like trying to sell a house in a falling market, regularly cutting prices, always a step behind the decline, chasing demand to the very bottom.

Revenues kept sliding as the virtuous cycles turned vicious and secondary effects multiplied. The drop in future investments, in customer confidence, and in company morale combined to drive huge declines in revenues in 2002. More write-offs were taken, more losses declared. More plants were closed and another 6,800 people were let go, including the chief executive, John Loose, and the leader of the company's largest division. Corning stock ended the year trading at less than 1 percent of its historic high.

With a last-minute influx of expensive new capital, Corning staved off concerns about bankruptcy and staggered into 2003. Management now maintains that it may be two or three more years before Corning can reignite growth. Good luck.

Fortunately, few businesses face the extreme challenges of Corning, but every low-growth organization must endure the debilitating effects of virtuous growth cycles running in reverse. Low growth leads to less reinvestment, lower customer confidence, and faltering employee morale. It is an aggressive disease.

Five Paths to Perdition

If high growth is the *sine qua non* of business success, as it surely is, then its elusiveness should come as no surprise. Whatever makes winners in a world of losers is bound to be hard to achieve. In fact, high growth is so slippery that its absence is not only epidemic among average businesses but also a constant threat to the most established corporations in the land. Let's sample the incidence of no-growth disease in the supposedly healthy universe of blue-chip enterprises.

Why are so many seemingly strong enterprises spiraling downward? Are they being replaced by "transformational companies," as some would have us believe? Do they represent aging business models doomed to be overtaken by a new generation of high-energy start-ups?

Actually, the degeneration of a major company is more often a case of self-destruction than of being lapped by a newer business model. Most decaying enterprises are brought down by their own managers, yoked to wishful thinking and dumb tactics that fail to deliver growth.

At Motorola, for example, three generations of Galvins have run the company for most of its seventy-five-year history, raising it from a tiny electric-transformer company to a multibillion-dollar enterprise. But since Chris Galvin, the grandson of the founder, assumed the helm at the beginning of 1997, the corporation's stock price has dropped by 85 percent. With sales shrinking an average of 2.5 percent a year, big losses have ensued. How could a leader of the wireless revolution get so bogged down?

Revlon is an even grimmer case. During one three-year stretch of billionaire Ron Perelman's ownership, Revlon's revenues dropped in every single quarter—twelve straight declines. Its stock recently traded for about 3 percent of its peak value in 2000—and its debt has been dropped to junk status. An enterprise that had dominated cosmetics counters for half a century is now fighting for relevance.

AT&T's Mike Armstrong, as I noted earlier, spent more than a fortune acquiring cable television, Internet access, and local-telephone businesses. What does he have to show for the money? Revenues and gross profits are lower than they were five years ago. Now, Armstrong is breaking up AT&T into its component parts, selling them one by one, and the only surviving fragment is providing long-distance phone service.

How does such appalling disintegration get started? How do organizations stop growing? There are five paths to perdition.

1. The company may have overexploited its franchise by neglecting *customer value* for years. If customers can't move to another supplier quickly, they will endure inferior value but only until they find a better option.

2. The company may have *placed a bad bet* on a market in which growth came to a screeching halt. Overinvested and overextended, the organization becomes vulnerable to competitors with greater financial resources and flexibility.

3. The company may have *lost a proprietary advantage*. Examples include the expiration of a patent, a compromise in a special distribution relationship, or the removal of regulatory protection.

4. The company may have *missed a significant value shift* in a marketplace. Customers whose buying had been based on product features are now focusing on price, or customers who had gone with low-price suppliers are now shifting to total-solution suppliers.

5. The company may have been *caught napping* by a new competitor with next-generation value. This is the rarest of the paths.

Which of these five problem areas afflicted Motorola, Revlon, and AT&T?

Don't blame Motorola's woes on the high-tech downturn. While Motorola was turning in a cumulative loss from 1997 to 2002, its closest competitor, Nokia, racked up profits of $14 billion and grew them during that period at an average annual compound rate of 17 percent. During that same period, as Motorola's revenues were declining, Nokia increased sales at an annual compound rate of 27 percent. Wireless communications has been a very good market to be in.

Clearly, Nokia caught Motorola's managers napping. Motorola thought its leading-edge technology could support sky-high prices for cell phones, but Nokia had another idea. Motorola also missed a significant market shift, as cell phones became fashion accessories with shortened life cycles and mass distribution requirements.

Most surprising, Motorola made an almost fatal misjudgment in technology. When cell phones shifted from analog to digital technology, Motorola was late to the party, surrendering sales momentum to Nokia and Ericsson. By 1998, digital phones were outselling analog devices, and Motorola's share of them was only 11.5 percent. Meanwhile, Nokia had scooped up 40 percent of the market and Ericsson had another 20 percent. Motorola still hasn't recovered.

Revlon was simply clueless in the face of competitors such as Estée Lauder, Unilever, and Johnson & Johnson's Neutrogena division. Perelman, who gained control of Revlon in a hostile takeover in 1985, gave the company a boost by hiring supermodel Cindy Crawford to be its spokeswoman and represent its image. But her heavy makeup went out of style, replaced by a more natural look that apparently escaped Revlon's notice.

Adding to Revlon's woes was the attrition of neighborhood drugstores, once the key to its cosmetic marketing. The cruelest cut of all came from younger customers such as twenty-five-year-old Zsuzsanna Vig, who declared in a *New York Times* article that Revlon's lipstick "smells like an old woman."

In 1999, Perelman brought in a new chief executive, Jeffrey Nugent from Neutrogena, to turn the corporation around. Nugent fired Crawford, but a new line of products did only moderately well; the Revlon image remained hopelessly dowdy. Another new CEO, Jack L. Stahl, arrived in 2002. Stahl, who came from outside the cosmetics business, was hired away from Coca-Cola on Perelman's hunch that a fresh outside eye might be clearer. Stahl said he is looking forward to "learning the dynamics of the industry."

AT&T had possibly the worst case of the no-growth disease: it made bad bets on new markets, lagged on customer value, milked the market until it dried up, and was caught napping by new competitors. Finally, it lost a proprietary advantage when new regulations allowed local phone companies to enter its long-distance market before AT&T had established itself as a primary provider of local service.

Armstrong admitted that his acquisition strategy and timing were badly off-target. In his words, he "didn't foresee the dot-com implosion, didn't foresee the telecom implosion or the economic recession." It may be unfair to blame him entirely for AT&T's loss to its new rivals. After all, charlatans at Qwest, Global Crossing, and other corporations were offering outstanding value to customers while paying little attention to the fact that they weren't turning profits.

Any company can temporarily lose its way and wander down one or another of the paths to perdition. It happens to the best of organizations from time to time, but the multitude of missteps at Motorola, Revlon, AT&T, and other such growth failures is indicative of haphazard and undisciplined growth management.

The Road to Double-Digit Growth

In my studies, the businesses that steadily delivered double-digit growth had guiding principles and management disciplines that stood in stark contrast to those at Motorola, Revlon, AT&T, and other no-growth and low-growth businesses.

The fundamental advantage of steadily growing companies is that they hedge their bets against the vicissitudes of an unpredictable world; they minimize risk by never putting all their eggs in one basket. For example, they don't allow the business to become dependent on one breakthrough, recognizing that it may have a short half-life, a brilliant patent, for example, whose lifetime is limited, or a dominant technology that may be outflanked, or a temporary monopoly susceptible to new regulations, or a price spike for an indispensable commodity that enrages customers and inevitably invites low-price competition. All such one-shot advantages create growth, yes, but mainly short-term growth spurts on narrow fronts that lull managers into a comatose state where they can be more easily blindsided or sandbagged by competitors.

By contrast, the steady-growth companies I studied were clearly protected by multifront strategies that kept them moving forward as a whole even when some fronts collapsed. Six key principles defined their approach to growth, enabling them to seize opportunities while minimizing risk. The six key principles are:

• *Spread the risk.* Every growth initiative has two potential sides, up and down, neither wholly predictable. If you depend on just one initiative, you have a high chance of failure. Accordingly, you need to hedge your bets by creating a portfolio of many initiatives that complement each other. In short, and as noted just above, diversify, diversify, diversify.

• *Take small bites.* Don't let double-digit growth become a challenge so huge that it seems unmanageable. Make it easy on yourself: decompose the problem. Set up smaller growth objectives in several complementary areas, and then exceed them. Don't choke on the double-digit challenge. Split it into small bites you can easily chew and swallow.

• *Balance your strategies.* You limit your potential if you grow your business mainly by organic expansion or by acquisitions. You progress faster when you recognize the complementary nature of these approaches and strive for a balance between the two. Organic and acquired growth have different strengths, and there is a time and a place for each.

• *Commit to superior value.* Nothing stops growth faster than an inferior value proposition; nothing spurs growth faster than a superior one. To foil competitors on every front, make sure you offer top value in all aspects of your business. Superior value makes everything easier. It's the key to retaining more customers, gaining greater market share, and penetrating more new markets.

• *Expand growth capabilities.* Management capacity, not market demand, is usually the binding constraint on growth. To loosen that bind, and grow at faster rates, focus first on your growth capabilities in deciding whether, where, and how to expand the enterprise. Your business won't grow if it lacks the operating capacity to grow.

• *Manage for growth.* Establish a distinct system for managing a growth portfolio through varied market conditions. The system should coordinate and focus all growth aspects, including attitudes, behavior, information, review processes, roles, and responsibilities. The purpose, needless to say, is to maximize growth as the common cause of every person and every unit of your organization.

These six growth principles underpin my portfolio approach to double-digit growth. To a degree, as we'll see in Chapter 9, the growth portfolio is similar to a diversified investment portfolio designed to risk capital in ways that can both increase and preserve it. Similarly, growth portfolios can be managed to improve the predictability of growth even though the underlying initiatives are inherently risky and unpredictable. The growth portfolio is based upon five growth disciplines.

1. The first discipline focuses on improving the company's customer-base retention. One of the easiest ways to improve growth is to slow the rate at which you lose your existing customers. As we'll see in Chapter 4, retaining customers requires much more than the simple loyalty programs employed by many organizations today.

2. The second growth discipline focuses on market share gain. This is usually the toughest, nastiest way to growth, because it requires

tearing customers away from a competitor. No company gives up market share without a struggle. In Chapter 5, we'll explore both organic and acquired market share growth initiatives.

3. The third discipline focuses on making sure you show up where growth is going to happen. Market positioning, when done right, is perhaps the easiest way to grow, because it requires little more than establishing a presence in the fastest-growing segments of a market and getting a decent piece of the action. As we'll see in Chapter 6, spotting those growth opportunities early and getting established with sufficient market share is a major challenge.

4. The fourth discipline focuses on penetrating adjacent markets. It requires a steely appraisal of whether your core operating capabilities can truly give you an advantage in an ancillary market, and whether your organization can build or acquire the additional capabilities needed to meet competitive standards in that market. In Chapter 7, we'll examine companies that have mastered those skills.

5. The fifth discipline focuses on achieving growth by invading new lines of business, where your core operating capabilities are of little advantage. As we'll see in Chapter 8, this discipline is built on smart investing rather than management skills. It's a growth discipline that few management teams are likely to master without further training and experience.

Double-Digit Growth Is a Choice

Hearing corporate managers explain away their growth problems is a little like listening to an addict in denial. Don't they understand that growth is a choice—a choice that lies entirely within their power and no one else's? Don't they realize that growing is a choice to succeed and not growing is a choice to fail?

Double-digit growth doesn't come free. A business doesn't grow because the economy permits it, the government subsidizes it, customers clamor for it, or a higher power shines its light upon it. In fact, hardly any of the forces you contend with really want you to grow, since your gain portends their loss.

Yet, double-digit growth is not a dream but a plausible scenario. The economy, though important, is but a small factor in the growth potential of any one company. Competition, though fierce, can be outfought and outflanked. Customers, though demanding, want to grow with value-creating suppliers.

If the challenge of double-digit growth appears a bit daunting, as it may to some readers, undaunt yourself and take heart. The beauty of the five growth disciplines is that any company is capable of carrying them out, consistent with its own particular ambitions and circumstances.

If that sounds like a promise—my value proposition for this book—you've heard right. In the next chapter, I offer a growth-discipline analysis of six corporations: Johnson Controls, Mohawk Industries, Paychex, Biomet, Oshkosh Truck, and Dell Computer. My hope is that their success will foreshadow your own organization's takeoff.

2

Who's Achieving
Double-Digit Growth?

How does all this work in real life? To find out, let's look at six diverse enterprises—Johnson Controls, Mohawk Industries, Paychex, Biomet, Oshkosh Truck, and Dell Computer—that have achieved notable growth by following a portfolio approach. In many respects, these organizations defy conventional wisdom. None of them grew, as some analysts would advise, by "transforming its business." They didn't get carried away by New Economy excesses. Most emphatically, they didn't succeed by abandoning the businesses that accounted for their original success.

In the race for growth, each of these organizations has played the tortoise, not the hare. They have demonstrated that growth can come from a variety of fields simultaneously, by steady one-step-at-a-time progress, rather than through high-risk, bet-your-company transformation schemes.

It's no accident that these companies have adopted a portfolio approach to growth. Using the five growth disciplines has freed these businesses from the constraints that limit so many other companies, and I believe these disciplines will work for any enterprise. Their cases demonstrate how the five disciplines complement each other, creating a powerful growth stream that carries along the whole organization.

Johnson Controls—Growing from Products to Solutions

In 1883, Warren S. Johnson, a professor at the State Normal School in Whitewater, Wisconsin, won a U.S. patent for the first electric room thermostat. Two years later, along with some local investors, he founded the Johnson Electric Service Company in Milwaukee to make, install, and service automatic temperature-regulation systems for buildings.

Over the next twenty-five years, Johnson's inventiveness continued. He developed electric storage batteries, steam-powered autos, and wireless telegraph equipment, but when he died in 1912, his company's management ignored all of those later creations and focused entirely on temperature controls.

Although it took a while, the professor would no doubt be pleased to learn that his business, renamed Johnson Controls, has lost its singular focus. To be sure, it has expanded and elaborated its building-control systems—they now enable customers to automate and remotely manage every aspect of their structures, from lighting and heating to access and equipment maintenance—but the corporation has also plunged into some very different markets, namely, automotive batteries and automotive interiors. And despite its unglamorous collection of businesses, it has achieved remarkable growth.

During 2002, Johnson had earnings of more than $650 million on sales of $20 billion. As of that year, it had increased sales for fifty-six consecutive years; boosted income for twelve consecutive years; and increased dividends for twenty-seven consecutive years. Since 1995, Johnson has lifted revenues by an average of 14 percent, gross profits by 13.5 percent, and net profits by a whopping 18.6 percent per year. As those figures suggest, Johnson has been a standout on growth, and it has done so by employing all five growth disciplines.

Let's consider them one by one.

Base Retention. The corporation has deployed a two-pronged strategy to retain its customer base: create service relationships that entangle customers in complex, hard-to-unwind relationships and deliver innovations that maintain market-leading customer value.

The "results-oriented services" offered in its building-controls division illustrate the company's customer-entanglement strategy. Not only can Johnson design and manufacture the systems; it can also install, maintain, and operate them with a full-time, on-site staff. The organization also provides performance contracting, enabling customers to upgrade their current control systems without any out-of-pocket costs. Customers' payments are generated by their savings in energy costs.

At CIBA Vision, a leading maker of soft contact lenses as well as eye pharmaceuticals in Duluth, Georgia, Johnson installed a computerized system to manage preventive and routine maintenance. It also provides a team to handle CIBA's overall facility-support service. CIBA's energy costs were cut by more than $100,000 a year, preventive-maintenance costs by $20,000 a year, and corrective-maintenance costs by 20 percent. In fact, in response to Johnson's ultimate value proposition—"we can do it all more effectively"—CIBA turned its whole facility-support operations over to Johnson. The intricacies of such relationships make customers very reluctant to change providers. It is a perfect base-retention strategy.

In its automotive-interiors division, customers have become dependent on—entangled with—Johnson Controls as partners on the path toward tomorrow's winning automobile designs. Johnson provides advanced market-research services to its largest automaker customers, helping them better understand the interior features that will drive vehicle sales. For example, Johnson's research has found that today's buyers want instrument panels filled with high-tech dials and controls, but that future buyers will want these functions hidden until they are needed. Other research indicates that customers for luxury vehicles have no desire for larger ones, but they do want more inside room, for which they will sacrifice trunk space.

Base retention demands constant improvement in the value proposition the organization presents customers, avoiding a value gap that attracts predatory competitors. From its origins in Professor Johnson's research laboratory to today, the corporation's business units have been consistently committed to product leadership.

Johnson's automated-control systems, for example, are state-of-the-art, backed by research facilities that produce a steady flow of innovations and are dedicated to promoting comfort while saving energy. Their product innovations have not just kept up with the industry—they have set the pace.

In its automotive-interiors division, the company continues to improve upon the value proposition of its car seats, the product that started Johnson in the industry. It maintains industry-leading research facilities in such areas as comfort, design ergonomics, noise control, safety, and consumer value in seats and other interior appointments. It has reengineered its "idea-to-showroom" process to dramatically reduce time to market, and it works closely with carmakers to find other ways to accelerate the pace of interior innovation.

In the automotive-battery business, too, Johnson Controls is the industry leader in product quality. It regularly develops new batteries that are smaller and lighter than the standard lead-plate battery and yield longer battery life. The latest model offers a 30 percent improvement in battery life over its predecessor.

Share Gain. Johnson Controls' product innovation has served to drive its market share gain as well as retain its base of customers. The company has relentlessly upped the ante on customer value, including sophisticated services, in every one of its businesses. Johnson's competitors have been forced to play catch-up.

The corporation has employed a remarkably consistent share-gain

strategy across its three different divisions. Johnson's value innovations in products and services have been targeted at ever-expanding
definitions of customers' problems. For example, in the building-
controls business, Johnson has innovated at the component level—
thermostats, switches, sensors, and the like. Also, it has innovated in
the design, installation, and maintenance of complete heating, venti-
lating, and air-conditioning systems. And it has created innovations
for complete building-control systems that include fire alarms, equipment monitoring, and security systems. It has even created innovations for entire real estate portfolios and large campus facilities.

Its Metasys software, for example, enables building managers to
check remotely on projects in any number of locations in one building
or several buildings. At Wake Forest University, a manager can track
equipment maintenance, adjust heating and air-conditioning, and
monitor fire sensors and security, all without leaving a central desk.
The savings in cost and improvements in performance are obvious.

At the component level, Johnson gained a head start on its competitors by rapidly adopting smart cards and biometrics technology,
then demonstrating how the cards could be used for a host of new applications. Johnson showed hospital staff how to use the cards to keep
track of defibrillators; now, the nearest one can be located instantly in
an emergency, allowing the hospital to keep fewer on hand. Moreover, the company has developed a smart-card–based security system
that protects nurses walking into a dark parking lot at night. Their
smart cards automatically turn on lights and cameras, and alert
guards, who may be on the opposite side of the lot, to watch them approach and enter their cars.

This multitiered approach to value innovation has two effects.
First, it gives Johnson a much broader playing field on which to up
the ante on its competition. By looking at every customer problem
through a telescoping lens, Johnson is able to open up a multifront
war on competitors. The second effect is to drive a shift in customer-

buying behavior toward broader and broader total solutions that few competitors are equipped to provide. And, of course, it also serves Johnson's purposes that at each higher level are greater customer spending and opportunities for growth.

Market Positioning. Over the years Johnson Controls has successfully improved its market position in each of its businesses, moving into fast-growing international markets and service areas through a combination of organic efforts and acquisitions. By expanding its definition of the customer problem and pushing into integrated services, the building-controls division has dramatically increased the size, growth rate, and profit margins of its potential market. Its base business, dependent upon new construction trends, cycles with the economy. But the services business, which addresses the needs of existing buildings, is significantly less cyclic and is able to carry a steadier and higher margin. Thus, Johnson has improved its position in a broad set of building services over the past decade and steadily grown through good times and bad.

To better position itself in faster-growing segments of the automotive-seating and automotive-batteries industries, Johnson has gone on a buying spree. Until a few years ago, it was principally a supplier to Detroit's Big Three carmakers, but more rapid growth opportunities were available with Japanese and European manufacturers that were still expanding at Detroit's expense. That's why, in 2000, Johnson bought Ikeda Bussan Co. Ltd., a Japanese manufacturer and Nissan's principal supplier of auto seats; Johnson wanted to be better positioned among the fast-growing Japanese automakers. Recently, it purchased the automotive business of Groupe Sagem, the French-based high-tech organization, to boost its position with European luxury automakers. Similarly, the company recently bought Varta and Hoppecke, two leading German auto-battery manufacturers, and it now claims the number-one spot in the European market.

These acquisitions actually straddle two growth disciplines: *market positioning* and *share gain*. They have advanced the organization in European and Asian markets, where it had previously occupied only a niche position. Furthermore, with the globalization of the automotive industry, carmakers now prefer to deal with fewer suppliers, who can meet their needs throughout the world. What had been separate geographic markets for, say, batteries, are fast becoming one big market. Thus, Johnson's purchases of European battery manufacturers and European and Japanese seat suppliers strengthened its hand in two ways: they provided an immediate boost in global market share while improving its value proposition for serving global automakers.

Adjacent-Market Penetration. Johnson's emphasis on integration, on finding new ways to combine its various skills and resources, has inevitably led the company to master the fourth growth discipline, penetrating adjacent markets. This restless organization never stops innovating.

Its building-control division has branched out from the installation and maintenance of building-control systems to the management of complete facilities, assigning a full-time, on-site staff to handle all of a building's operating and maintenance needs. About fifteen years ago, Johnson spotted this adjacent market as a natural growth opportunity, where the company could leverage its building expertise for real advantage. The following year, Johnson entered the market, wisely acquiring a business that could provide the basic operating capabilities that it lacked. Today, Johnson Controls is the world leader in managing complex buildings, such as pharmaceutical laboratories and trophy headquarters.

Its expertise in temperature-control systems also inspired Johnson to penetrate the market for security systems for nonresidential buildings. Before long, the corporation was ready to leverage its new security expertise to invade neighboring markets. Airport security was a natural fit, and the company now provides that service to some thirty U.S. airports. In fact, its airport-security skills are so well honed that, in 2001, it won a contract from the U.S. Federal Aviation Administration (FAA) to deliver security-system integration to 925 air-traffic–control facilities.

In a similar way, the automotive-interiors division has entered markets adjacent to its core seating business. In fewer than ten years, these moves have transformed the division from a supplier of seating to a creator of complete automotive interiors. Laden with complex electronics that cost several times as much as the entire frame and body, as well as creature comforts such as heated and cooled seating, the interiors are where the money is to be found in automobile design.

Johnson greatly expanded its capabilities in that area with the 1996 acquisition of Prince Automotive, which produced door panels and consoles, and the 1998 purchase of the Becker Group, which turned out instrument panels. Today, the company acquires the components it doesn't make and delivers complete interiors to the carmakers' assembly plants in synch with the vehicles' movement along the assembly line.

Johnson Controls' move into automotive interiors illustrates its acute understanding of adjacent-market penetration. It designs, develops, and validates all of the components that go into its interiors, but it doesn't make the specialized electronics or many of the commodity parts, for which it has manufacturing partners, such as Jabil Circuit and Yazaki of Japan. It doesn't want to make mainstream commodity products because their profit margins are relatively unattractive. Instead, its objective is to control the entire automotive interior, manufacturing only those components that provide differentiated value, through either unique consumer features or reduced integration costs.

A major new product being developed by Johnson would solve a real problem for automakers and enable the company to achieve major expansion in an adjacent market. Since it usually takes at least three years to carry a new car from concept to assembly line, while electronics innovations appear every six months or so, cars are often built with outdated electronic systems. Johnson is trying to create a single electronic system that could adapt to last-minute changes, or, as one executive put it, "reconcile the clock speed of the auto industry with the clock speed of the electronics industry." This plug-and-play design is intended to be a model, not just for a single organization, but for the industry as a whole.

Another adjacent-market penetration that is high on the company's product agenda is to expand under the hood of an automobile. First up is a battery module made of injection-molded plastic, designed to contain, along with the battery, such nearby systems as radiator-overflow tanks and windshield-washer-fluid containers. Such a module would save space under the hood as well as reduce automakers' production and assembly costs. What's more, if all goes as planned, Johnson will soon enhance the system with its electronics expertise, thus creating the first intelligent-battery system. It will give drivers a status report on the battery's function and expected life.

In other words, Johnson is using its strong market position in batteries to create adjacent growth in other under-the-hood modules. This simultaneously strengthens its core battery business and opens up new room for growth. Brilliant.

At the same time, Johnson is supporting an industrywide shift to forty-two-volt systems under the hood. This significant technological change will pave the way for the replacement of mechanical systems for steering and braking with electronic systems. Are Johnson's planners plotting the organization's expansion into complete electromechanical systems for driving control?

The lesson to learn from Johnson Controls is this: if you develop and acquire enough resources in enough aspects of a particular market, your potential for penetrating nearby markets is enormously enhanced.

New Lines of Business. Johnson Controls is one of the few veteran practitioners of this fifth growth discipline. It entered both the automotive-battery business and the automotive-interiors business through acquisitions of companies unrelated to anything going on in the organization at the time.

In 1978, the company bought Globe-Union, a manufacturer of automotive batteries based in Wisconsin. Today, Johnson is the largest manufacturer of private-label, lead-acid car batteries in North America, selling to retailers such as AutoZone and Sears, as well as to automakers. In 1985, Johnson acquired Hoover Universal, a Michigan-based producer of car seats. Today, Johnson makes more completed vehicle seats than any company in the world and is the largest supplier of automotive interiors.

Johnson has managed to build powerful new divisions that are sustaining the company's enviable record of growth, while avoiding the dangers inherent in moving away from core capabilities.

Several traits have propelled Johnson Controls to success in each of the growth disciplines. First, the company's core strength derives from an unwavering commitment to customer-value leadership. This is an organization that believes that research and innovation are the engines of growth. Next, the corporation has long held that product and service businesses are equally important; at Johnson Controls, service doesn't take a backseat to product sales. That has aided the corporation in creating an ever-expanding view of the customer opportunity. At each level, products and services are combined to create innovative, value-creating offerings that are entirely new to the market. Finally, Johnson Controls has struck a balance between organic and acquired growth. It understands where acquisitions can be used to advance a market position or gain needed capabilities, and it integrates those acquisitions seamlessly.

Mohawk Industries—Something for Everyone

A 120-year-old carpet manufacturer based in Calhoun, Georgia, Mohawk Industries began its present-day life as a spin-off of Mohasco in 1988, and it was taken public again in 1992. It worked the way leveraged buyouts are supposed to work. At the time, Mohawk had sales of $300 million with a 3 percent share of the carpet market.

Eleven years later, it is a $4.5 billion supplier of flooring for homes, offices, and other commercial space, with products including broadloom, rugs, ceramic tiles, laminate, wood, and vinyl flooring and such brand names as Karastan, Bigelow, Mohawk, and Dal-Tile.

What about Mohawk's growth credentials? They are impressive. Each year, from 1997 to 2002, its revenues rose an average of 12.4 percent; gross profits, an average of 17.2 percent; and net income, an average of 29 percent.

Base Retention. Mohawk sells all its products through distributors—flooring dealers for commercial sales; specialty retailers, home centers, and mass merchants for consumers. Since end customers buy flooring so infrequently, and the distributors determine which of the many competing products they will carry, Mohawk's base-retention strategy goes something like this: keep distributors happy, and you'll keep the end customer. How do you keep your distributors happy? You help build their profits.

Home Depot, Sears, and Target all, at various times, have named Mohawk their Vendor of the Year because of its focus on quality, logistics (especially its fast turnaround time on orders), in-store displays, and training (especially its Mohawk University, the most extensive retail training system in the industry). Mohawk is number one among specialty retailers and flooring dealers for the same reasons, though they benefit from different Mohawk programs designed for their unique needs.

Share Gain. In 1992, Mohawk was a $300 million niche player in the high and middle ends of the flooring business. It had a 3 percent share of the total market. Since then, Mohawk has used both internal growth and acquisition to gain a 28 percent share of the $12 billion market.

"On the internal growth side," according to Jeffrey S. Lorberbaum, president and chief executive officer, "we've grown at about twice the industry average. The growth was fueled by broadening our product line so we can fulfill all customer needs, supported by low-cost state-of-the-art manufacturing."

In broadening its product line, Mohawk has made extensive efforts to keep its designs and colors in synch with home-fashion trends. The company's scouts scrutinize the furniture market, analyze new fabrics, and study trends in wall and window treatments. It also maintains the Asheville Design Council, a group of architects and designers who alert the company to new developments. These and other efforts allow Mohawk to spot trends early and get its products out ahead of competition.

The corporation has also gained share from competitors directly— by buying them out. For example, in 1999 Mohawk acquired Durkan Patterned Carpets for $116 million to increase its market share in the hotel-carpeting segment. Lorberbaum has said that Mohawk has bought thirteen corporations since going public. "What we look for in acquisitions," he added, "are North American businesses where we can leverage the customer, the distribution and the manufacturing assets. All thirteen of the acquisitions were accretive to earnings in the first year."

Market Positioning. Mohawk's trend-spotting skills have also enabled the company to make some important market-positioning moves. Recognizing the increasing numbers of consumers devoted to environmental causes, Mohawk decided to provide a product tailored to their beliefs. In 1999, the corporation acquired Image Industries, a recycler, and the following year it launched Enviro-Tech, a line of carpeting made entirely of recycled plastic bottles. Since then, Mohawk has become one of the largest soda-bottle recyclers in the United States, handling two billion bottles a year.

Mohawk produces an extraordinarily broad line of products to continuously enhance its positioning within every segment of the flooring market, from the least expensive synthetic rolls to the most luxurious, hand-cut wool carpeting. To accommodate such a range, the organization maintains no fewer than a dozen distinct brands and sub-brands, each targeted toward a different consumer- or commercial-buying segment.

The company has also used licensing agreements with designers— including Ralph Lauren, Tommy Hilfiger, Joe Boxer, and, yes, even Martha Stewart—to reach into specialty segments of the carpet and rug market. For Ralph Lauren the company built a store-within-a-store boutique to demonstrate how Mohawk products coordinated with the furniture fabric and wall coverings of the Lauren line.

Adjacent-Market Penetration. Mohawk recognizes that it has two core advantages that can help it seize share in adjacent markets: its strong distribution channel relationships and its knowledge of color and style trends in flooring.

The corporation moved into vinyl flooring in 2000 with an agreement to distribute Congoleum products. Congoleum is one of the largest and best-recognized manufacturers of vinyl tiles and linoleum. Mohawk chose to enter this business as a distributor rather than as a manufacturer because the vinyl market is brutally competitive and amounts to only $2 billion in total annual U.S. sales.

In March 2002, Mohawk completed the acquisition of Dal-Tile International, the largest U.S. supplier of ceramic tile, though it produces the tiles in Monterrey, Mexico. Mohawk paid $1.8 billion, half of it with cash from operations. At the time, Dal-Tile had approximately $1 billion in annual sales.

Mohawk's rationale was explained by its CEO, Lorberbaum: "Dal-Tile has about a 26 percent share of the ceramic business, which is about four times that of their next competitor. They have the strongest brands in the ceramic business with unmatched distribution similar to Mohawk's. They are the only ceramic provider that has a full line of wall tile, floor tile, stone, and other ceramic products needed to support the entire business."

New Lines of Business. None. For the foreseeable future, Mohawk has all the growth it can handle in its core flooring business.

Paychex—Flying Under the Radar

Thomas Golisano founded Paychex in 1971 with $3,000 in startup capital, one employee, forty customers, and a simple idea: provide payroll processing for small businesses. At the time, processors such as ADP were focused on large employers of fifty or more. Golisano flew under their radar, pursuing businesses with just five, ten, or thirty employees and charging them as little as $5 per pay period to start.

As of 2002, Paychex provided payroll services to more than 440,000 small businesses, and a variety of other services as well. Its revenues that year were $955 million with profits of $275 million. The company made Golisano a billionaire, which has enabled him to underwrite a couple of quixotic campaigns to become governor of New York.

Paychex has also done well by its investors. Between 1997 and 2002, it has seen an increase in dividends every single year and eight stock splits. During that time, the company also boasted average annual gains in revenues of 19 percent, gross profit increases of 20.9 percent, and net income gains of 29.6 percent. Since many of Paychex's costs are fixed, income continues to grow at a faster pace than revenues.

Base Retention. More than 95 percent of all U.S. businesses have fewer than fifty employees. That's Paychex's primary market; its customers average only fourteen employees. The owners of these businesses are fed up with the hassles of bookkeeping and tax filing, not to mention all those federal employment regulations, such as TEFRA, COBRA, and ERISA. But they tend to be reluctant to outsource these operations because they know that payroll or compliance mistakes can cause havoc. And if they do decide to hire outside help, they want to know that someone will always be on call, twenty-four/seven, if a problem arises.

Tom Golisano knows these customers intimately, and he knows what is needed to keep them happy. As he puts it, "Our customers are looking for peace of mind." And the way he provides it is via his employee training program.

Sure, Paychex has huge computer systems for grinding out the paperwork, but Golisano knows that they can't deliver quality service; only his people can do that. So every employee receives an average of 150 hours of training each year, and sixteen of the programs are on a high enough level to be certified for college credit.

Golisano has also configured the organization to be close to its customers. Paychex operates out of one hundred separate regional centers dedicated to serving customers in their particular areas. Each client is assigned a regular service representative, and most reps interact with their clients on a weekly basis. It's a high-touch operation with a high-tech back end.

Of course, customers also stay put because the company delivers on the high-tech side. Paychex has been nationally recognized for its service quality in payroll processing and pension-plan record-keeping, and the Internal Revenue Service (IRS) has hailed the corporation for its exceptional participation in the agency's electronic tax-filing initiatives.

Share Gain. According to *Forbes* estimates, Paychex holds a 70 percent share of the small-business payroll-processing market. That sounds like market saturation, but there is still room to grow. According to Golisano, 85 percent of small businesses have yet to outsource their payroll processing.

Since its founding in 1971, Paychex has increased market share principally through internally generated improvements in its no-hassle value proposition. That has brought in some of those bashful businesses as well as corralling customers from Paychex's few competitors.

As for that other road to share gain, acquisitions, the organization's only notable purchase was made in 2002 when it bought a competitor, Advantage Payroll Services, a privately owned payroll processor, for $314 million. Advantage serviced the small-business owner and had about forty-nine thousand customers, and it added about 10 percent to Paychex's customer base.

"We feel we can control growth better by growing internally," Golisano said not long ago. "There are risks to making acquisitions. Also, there isn't a large opportunity to make acquisitions in the payroll-processing arena."

Market Positioning. Back in 1971, Paychex essentially created a market segment that was ready to take off. It has done so, with no end in sight. The company's only serious competition comes from the efforts of small businesses to manage their own payroll processing, and there are signs that even that is waning. Given its dominant market position and growing market, Paychex only needs to hold on to its 70 percent share and watch its customer base float higher with the rising tide.

Paychex has engaged in two forms of market positioning over the years. Most importantly, it has enlarged its target area, serving businesses that employ between fifty and five hundred people. As of 1998, the company had revenues of only $13 million in this segment, but by 2002, they had soared to $100 million. In that year alone, revenues from the segment rose 50 percent.

Paychex has also expanded geographically into all major U.S. metropolitan markets. The organization shows little interest in positioning itself in international markets. "In many foreign countries," Golisano has noted, "the payroll problem is nowhere as difficult as it is in the U.S. Also, we have such an untapped market here at home, there is no need to go abroad for growth."

Adjacent-Market Penetration. Some of Paychex's growth is now created by carefully positioning the company in an expanding array of adjacent employer services that can be effectively sold to existing customers. As Golisano said a couple of years ago, "We have a very straightforward formula for growth . . . to increase the size of our client base by 11 percent to 12 percent a year. Then we have developed an array of ancillary products to go along with our core payroll product, such as 401(k) reporting and cafeteria-benefit plans. This combination enables us to grow our revenues over 20 percent a year."

The core service offering is called Taxpay. It is used by more than 85 percent of all Paychex customers to calculate and deposit taxes and file returns with appropriate governments and agencies. From there, companies can choose to pay employees totally on their own or use Paychex to provide checks and electronic deposits, or load the money onto Visa cards.

Next to these core services lie other employer services, such as retirement benefits and insurance that have separate and distinct competitors, capabilities, and cost structures. Paychex has successfully found growth by penetrating several of these adjacent markets. It introduced 401(k) pension record-keeping, workers compensation insurance, group insurance, and even a "co-employment" service whereby Paychex does all the work of a human-resources department.

In each of these adjacent markets, Paychex leverages three core advantages: strong and trusting customer relationships, efficient back-office processing, and an aggressive sales culture. The sales force has demonstrated its ability to move ancillary products. In 1997, fewer than 29 percent of its customers paid for services other than direct payroll. By the end of 2002, that figure had climbed to 65 percent.

The rationale for pushing such products was nicely summed up by Brandt Sakakeeny of Deutsche Bank: "The ancillary sale is an easy one, and has a much higher profit margin than the initial payroll sale. You already have the customer, all you need to do is pick up the phone."

New Lines of Business. Paychex can certainly afford to enter new lines of business. After all, it has such a surplus of cash that it is able to pay out more than 50 percent of its earnings in dividends each year. But its management sees no reason to roam, given the great opportunities still available in the company's core and adjacent markets.

Biomet—Implant Impresario

Warsaw, Indiana, is an unlikely spot for "the orthopedic capital of the world," but one company, Biomet, has made that claim credible. Founded by Dane Miller and three colleagues in 1977, Biomet rode the market for orthopedic implants to 2002 profits of $240 million on sales of $1.2 billion. Over the past fifteen years, sales have increased at a compound annual rate of 25 percent and earnings have risen 27 percent.

Chairman Miller describes his company in these terms: "Our principal product offering is total joint replacement, primarily total hips and total knees; that is about 60 percent of our revenue stream. But, in addition, we produce spinal products, dental reconstructive implants, arthroscopic sports medicine products, bone cements and accessories, operating room supplies, soft goods, and trauma products. We produce a very broad product offering and distribute the products in over one hundred countries throughout the world."

Miller earned his doctorate from the University of Cincinnati and then went on to research management jobs at an orthopedic division of Bristol-Myers Squibb and a subsidiary of Bayer. His cofounders were also industry veterans.

Biomet holds almost 10 percent of the $11 billion orthopedics market worldwide. An investment of $2,000 in its 1981 initial public offering was worth approximately $1 million at the end of 2002. From 1997 to 2002, its revenues grew at an average annual rate of 13.8 percent; gross profits, 15.3 percent; and net income, 16.9 percent.

Base Retention. Here's a simple statistic that probably explains everything one needs to know about Biomet's base-retention strategy: a Biomet employee is present at 95 percent of the operations involving its products. Hip and knee replacement surgery is complicated, and, as *Forbes* reports, "When a surgeon stalls in front of the dizzying array of instruments he must use in the operation, a Biomet representative guides him with the red dot of a laser pointer."

Customer support is a vital part of the value proposition for Biomet, along with the safety, reliability, and durability of its products. Its customers don't care all that much about cost. Cheap but shoddy substitute joints that fail once implanted in the body and must be replaced end up costing more than the pricey versions. The constantly improving quality of its products has enabled the company to keep its customers close to home.

Share Gain. Since its founding, Biomet has been a product innovator. It was among the first to use stronger, lighter, longer-lasting titanium alloys in total joint replacement. It pioneered the use of a porous surface coating to promote bone growth—the process is called plasma spray coating.

Two decades ago, the plastic implants used to replace cartilage and some bones were made in a multistep process that involved a considerable amount of molding and grinding. Biomet started casting the parts in a single step from polyethylene powder, a process that made for more durable implants.

Such product innovations have been a major element in the company's ability to gain new customers at the expense of its competitors. In addition to such organic growth, Biomet has also gone the acquisition route to achieve share-gain, market-positioning, and adjacent-market growth.

In November 1994, for example, the company increased its share of the joint replacement market, especially in Europe, with the purchase of Kirschner Medical. In January 1998, Biomet further bolstered its European presence by entering into a European joint venture with Merck. This has been a happy marriage, giving Biomet access to Merck's technology and Merck access to Biomet's reputation and distribution system in orthopedics.

Market Positioning. Orthopedic surgery requires a host of different products, creating a host of niche market segments. Biomet has been particularly skillful at spotting promising new niches and moving rapidly to get in on the ground floor. It has gained a top-four position in eleven different segments of the market for orthopedic products, and is number one or two in seven of those segments.

Biomet enjoys all the benefits of gaining favorable positions in a number of growing market segments, with its sales and profits rising along with the segments themselves. Two of the niches where it shines are the markets for hip- and knee-replacement surgery. Implants for these two procedures are now a $3.1 billion market opportunity, expanding about 15 percent annually.

The company has employed a combination of internal innovations and acquisitions to further its market positioning. For example, in May 1984, three years after the young company went public, it acquired Orthopedic Equipment Company, giving Biomet its first substantial presence in the large European market. The acquisition also broadened the product line in internal devices for stabilizing bone fractures.

In January 1988, Biomet bought Electro-Biology, instantly adding two new market segments to its skein: external fixation and electrical bone-growth stimulation. External fixation devices are used for complicated trauma, limb-lengthening, and deformity correction, as well as the repair of fractures. The stimulation products are machines that send electrical impulses through the bone to promote healing. The company is now number one in both segments. Since the acquisition, Biomet has particularly strengthened Electro-Biology's share of the $1.4 billion spinal products market, which is growing 18 to 20 percent per year.

Adjacent-Market Penetration. Biomet has made only one move beyond the orthopedic market, and even then it was close by. In December 1999, the company acquired Implant Innovations, a Palm Beach, Florida, enterprise that specializes in dental implants. The $300 million U.S. market for these implants is growing 15 percent a year, and the acquisition instantly made Biomet the number-two player.

Dental implants share many technological features with orthopedic implants. Biomet saw an opportunity to use its core technology skills to improve the acquired company's products and expand its growth horizons in this lucrative and growing market.

New Lines of Business. None. With its track record of growth, why look elsewhere?

Oshkosh Truck—Wheels Within Wheels

Since 1917, Oshkosh Truck has built vehicles that can withstand the most severe conditions and environments—specialty trucks and truck bodies for fire departments, the military, concrete placement, and refuse hauling. They roll under the Oshkosh, Pierce, McNeilus, Geesink, Norba, and Medtec brand names.

In 2002, the company generated sales of $1.7 billion and, since 1997, has grown revenue and profits at compound annual rates of 20.6 and 42.9 percent, respectively.

When Robert G. Bohn was hired as the head of operations in 1992 from—guess where—Johnson Controls, Oshkosh had one big customer, the U.S. Department of Defense, and revenues of less than $400 million. Since Bohn took over as chief executive in November 1997, revenues have tripled and the stock price has quadrupled. Also in those years, revenues have risen an average annual rate of 19 percent; gross profits, 20.9 percent; and net income, 29.6 percent. Oshkosh is a remarkable story of fast growth in slow markets.

Base Retention. Oshkosh's claim to fame is that it builds the world's toughest trucks and some of the biggest, as well. Parked beside the medium-sized trucks that Oshkosh builds for the U.S. and U.K. military, for example, a Humvee is a mere puppy dog. The ability to work under the most severe climatic conditions and over the roughest terrain is the company's calling card with military and commercial customers alike.

Oshkosh customers generally buy trucks through a bidding process that allows the incumbent little advantage. Thus, the key to its enviable levels of repeat purchase has been one thing—superior customer value. Base retention in its market is about winning the customers' business again and again and again.

One indication of the company's ability to deliver that value is that Oshkosh became the first truck manufacturer ever honored with the Department of Defense's highest recognition for acquisition excellence, the David Packard Award.

"Ultimately, the success of a diversified company comes down to the quality of its operating management," noted analyst Robert F. McCarthy Jr. of Robert W. Baird & Company, "and Oshkosh has a strong team." That view is echoed by David Kern, executive vice president of Kern Capital Management: "It's just a superbly run company."

Share Gain. Oshkosh has consistently grown market share in military vehicles, cement haulers, and fire apparatus using a common value strategy in each division. First, overwhelm the competition with new-product introductions. Next, create a lean cost structure that allows each vehicle to be custom-built at an affordable price. Third, continue to strengthen the distribution network of one hundred company-owned and authorized dealers and service facilities. The result: constant share gain at its rivals' expense.

Oshkosh's roots as a product innovator go way back. It was the company that pioneered the four-wheel–drive concept and the first to design aircraft rescue and firefighting vehicles.

More recently, the organization unveiled a revolutionary new diesel-electric propulsion technology, known as ProPulse, that is designed specifically for heavy trucks. In this system, the diesel engine powers a large electric generator, which provides direct power to the wheels, eliminating the torque converter, automatic transmission, transfer case, and drive shafts. In addition to being simpler, the system can deliver fuel economies of greater than 20 percent.

In cement mixers, the company has introduced the first-ever composite ready-mix drum, which weighs two thousand pounds less than a comparable steel drum. It allows cement companies to haul a larger payload, gaining greater productivity than other cement mixers. Innovation in vehicle design "continues to be a critical strategy for maintaining a leadership position," according to CEO Bohn.

Oshkosh has learned how to effectively transfer innovations among its divisions. The all-wheel steering developed for its military trucks, for example, is now available on its fire engines, and an onboard computer network used to simplify the connections between various fire truck systems is now in use in military vehicles. That kind of heads-up operation has given the company a big advantage in stealing customers from competitors.

Market Positioning. In 2001, Oshkosh took its first step to position itself in international markets. It paid $128 million in cash for Geesink Norba Group, a Dutch maker of garbage trucks. The company had $120 million of revenue and gave Oshkosh a 20 percent share of the European refuse-equipment industry and an attractive dealer network. The company plans to use that network to sell and service Oshkosh's other truck lines. Michael L. Grimes, CEO of one of Oshkosh's competitors in the military market, ridiculed that idea. "If I thought I was in the military business," he said, "I don't know that I'd go to Europe and buy a garbage-truck company." Given its track record, though, I'd hesitate to bet against Oshkosh.

Adjacent-Market Penetration. This is the growth discipline where Oshkosh really shines. It has used acquisitions to penetrate adjacent markets where it can make the most of its technology, manufacturing know-how, and distribution system.

Before 1996, Oshkosh was principally a military truck supplier. Bohn was the company's head of strategic planning. "We looked in the mirror," he said, "and asked: 'What are we?'" The analysis led to a decision to invade adjacent markets for complex, custom vehicles similar to the military vehicles the corporation already sold. Management also decided to penetrate those markets through acquisitions, and that it was safer to acquire the market leader.

In 1996, Oshkosh bought Pierce Manufacturing, one of the many competitors in the overcrowded market for fire apparatus. Bohn took over the division as soon as it was acquired and began a program of integration and improvement. Ten new products were introduced in the next two years, quite an improvement for an organization known more for quality and reliability than for innovation. Bohn also focused on improving manufacturing efficiencies, gaining ISO 9001 certification for quality, management, and installing twenty-four/seven customer service. For the first time, chief engineers were required to carry beepers so that they would be instantly accessible to a dealer trying to get a critical piece of equipment back in use. The company now claims about 25 percent of the U.S. market for fire trucks.

Two years later, Oshkosh bought its way into the cement-hauler and garbage-truck businesses with the $218 million acquisition of McNeilus. That company had revenues of $313 million and a market share in cement haulers of greater than 50 percent. As it did in the Pierce acquisition, Oshkosh immediately installed a company veteran as president of the new division, in this case removing Denzil Mc-Neilus, son of the founder. Bohn said his appointee's experience gave him "an excellent perspective to seamlessly integrate the operations to achieve corporate objectives."

The acquisition strategy for adjacent-market penetration has completely transformed Oshkosh's growth opportunities and mix of businesses. The company now boasts three major operating units; its sales of commercial trucks and emergency vehicles have actually surpassed those of military vehicles, its original product.

New Lines of Business. With 20 percent annual growth, international expansion yet ahead, and lots of other truck segments to enter,

Oshkosh hasn't shown the least bit of interest in investing outside its core.

Dell—Steady Results from a *Wunderkind*

The skeptics have had a field day with Dell Computer. Sure, they say, Michael Dell, the *wunderkind,* saw a market that no one else perceived and used his highly efficient, direct-sale business model to become the leading provider of home computers. But that was a while ago. Now, he is stuck with a commoditized personal-computer market that no one else wants, and his direct-sale model will never work with more complex goods or in overseas markets. So Dell's glory days are over, right?

Wrong. Michael Dell hears that theory often, he told me, and it alternately exasperates, infuriates, and amuses him. Critics have underestimated him since he started his enterprise in his college dorm room, then dropped out of school to build a business colossus. "People doubted us then, they doubt us now," he commented. Then, with his soft-spoken enthusiasm, he added, "I say, bring them on. We're coming right at them."

Like the Edgar Allan Poe character who hid his purloined letter in plain sight, Dell has an open secret of success. Though he repeatedly tells people the secret, they continue to ignore him, thinking it is too simple to be accurate. It is merely that Dell—the company and the founder—*likes* the commodity business. When executives think "commodity," Kevin Rollins, president and chief operating officer, said, their lips curl into sneers. He doesn't understand why. "Wal-Mart is a commodity retailer, [and it] blows the doors off other retailers," he said. "We believe we sell great products, and the market wants to buy them." So, Dell plans to go right on commoditizing the computer industry, piece by piece, while it keeps growing faster than anyone expects.

A couple of very different developments have affected the computer hardware industry of late. To begin with, the markets for computer and communications technologies abruptly and unexpectedly contracted in 2001 and 2002. This caused Dell to record its first-ever drop in sales, after enjoying more than a decade of annual growth greater than 25 percent. At the same time, these markets have been transforming and they are commoditizing.

Dell Computer has anticipated this transformation, has adjusted its growth strategy, and is once again growing at double-digit rates. In 2002, Dell's revenues climbed about 14 percent, while its nearest competitors were contracting. It grew gross and net profits even faster.

The shift in Dell's growth strategy to accommodate a changing market is one of the great stories of practical yet visionary management. Let's examine how Dell has adjusted each of its growth disciplines and why the company believes it will double revenues to $70 billion within five years.

Base Retention. In a commodity business, base retention is built on delivering the best value. Understanding that low prices are never low enough, Michael Dell relentlessly drives his organization toward greater operating efficiency in order to finance improvements in customer value.

As competitors try to emulate his efficient direct-to-customer, build-to-order business model, Dell has enlisted his major suppliers in a just-in-time supply chain revolution. The company has extended its legendary efficiency to its supplier base and fully integrated its members into one seamless product pipeline. And Dell never stops pushing for even more efficiency. Early in 2002, one Texas plant was turning out 30 percent more products than it had eighteen months earlier—and doing it in half the floor space.

Since nearly all these cost savings are passed on, there is little wonder that Dell's customers remain loyal. The company has maintained its gross profit margin at about 18 percent while Gateway, using the same direct-sales business model, has seen gross margins sink to 14 percent. In a price war, Gateway is at a serious disadvantage.

Dell has been just as relentless in managing operating expenses such as sales and marketing and R&D. In 2002, while sales rose $3.5 billion from two years earlier, Dell actually reduced its annual operating costs by $160 million, to 9.9 percent of revenues. In contrast, operating costs at Hewlett-Packard and Gateway come to 22 percent and 26 percent of revenues, respectively.

These efficiency differences have allowed Dell to turn up the heat on competitors with rock-bottom pricing. Competitors can match many of Dell's profitable prices only by selling at a loss. That is how to drive base retention in a relentlessly competitive marketplace while simultaneously driving your competitors out of business.

For large corporate customers, low prices often aren't enough. They also require sophisticated services to ensure that their total cost of ownership is the lowest it can be. In this and other important commercial segments, Dell provides efficient Web-based services and specialized sales and service personnel while constantly refining its business model to ensure that it is the best value in every segment in which it competes.

Share Gain. Through all of the high-tech turmoil of recent years, Dell has continued to gain share at the expense of its rivals. But this is hardly a new story; for all his affability, Michael Dell is feared throughout the industry as a fierce competitor.

In the technology slump of 2001, he didn't hesitate to start a devastating price war in the personal-computer market. When the blood was washed away, Dell was the only major personal-computer maker that had gained share profitably. It had overtaken Compaq as the market leader, sending that company into a merger with Hewlett-Packard. Gateway had to lay off 16 percent of its workforce, and mighty IBM abandoned the consumer market altogether. The personal-computer market produced a 10 percent drop in sales in that year, but Dell actually achieved an 18.3 percent increase in PC unit sales, which held its revenue decline to only 2 percent. According to Dataquest, its market share rose by 5 percent in the United States and 2.6 percent worldwide, bringing it to 13.3 percent. Michael Dell promptly announced that his company was aiming for a lot more.

Market Positioning. The success of Michael Dell's company can also be attributed to his skill at this third growth discipline. Despite the all-but-universal agreement that Dell's direct-sale model could not work in overseas markets, the company's expansion into markets outside the United States has been sensational. In every market in the world in which it competes, Dell is growing at a significantly higher multiple than the industry. In six foreign markets, the company has a 15 to 25 percent market share, representing about 45 percent of total overseas demand. In the other 55 percent of the overseas market, where Dell has not concentrated its efforts, it has about a 5 percent share.

All in all, international markets still account for only about one third of Dell's sales. That compares to 58 percent of Hewlett-Packard's revenue that was registered internationally. But the gap is closing fast, especially in the six foreign markets that have Dell's attention. For example, in Asia Pacific in 2002, Dell grew shipments by 42 percent. Not counting Dell, the whole region only grew shipments by 7 percent. In a single year, Dell jumped from sixth to third place among PC competitors in this region. In France, Dell grew shipments by 32 percent. The rest of the industry saw volume declines.

Geographic expansion will continue to be a big part of Dell's market growth future. At some point, those other international markets that Dell ignores will surely become a part of its plan for growth.

Adjacent-Market Penetration. Dell's growth ambitions are not limited to the personal computer marketplace. The company believes that it is well positioned to enter any large high-tech marketplace that is commoditizing—an exercise of the fourth discipline, penetrating adjacent markets. Says Michael Dell, "If you look at all the sectors—PCs, storage, software, peripherals, printers, networking—we have 3 percent market share across that, on average. So we have plenty of room to grow profitably, even if overall tech spending doesn't grow." Having moved into the server-computer and storage-systems markets, Dell is building its network device business and a printer division that will attack Hewlett-Packard's 50 percent share, and has powerfully expanded its computer support services offerings, as well.

The strategy is familiar: Dell has patiently waited for others to develop a market and then moved in when the time became ripe. The company learned from its ill-fated entry into the hotly competitive notebook market, from which it fled in 1993. At the time, Michael Dell agonized over the decision. All the experts were arguing that no serious player in the computer game could do without notebooks. Dell's mistake was that he entered the market too soon, before it began to commoditize.

Otherwise, the company's moves into adjacent markets have been a remarkable success. Already, it has come from nowhere to become the leading seller of server computers in the United States and number two in the world. And in partnership with EMC, the leading maker of enterprise-storage devices, Dell has launched a co-branding arrangement that gives it entrée into the $15 billion midrange information storage market. That venture built sales to a run rate of just over $1 billion by the end of 2002. That helped Dell to increase its external storage sales by 87 percent in 2002. EMC must be elated that its agreement with Dell has another four years to run.

Another company that should be looking over its shoulder is Cisco. Dell has quietly built a business selling networking devices—

routers, hubs, and the software for managing complex network communications—starting with products for small and medium-sized businesses. It entered the market in October 2001 and by July 2002 was announcing switching products that cost as little as one fifth the price of similar equipment from Cisco and 3Com. Two months later, Cisco cancelled an agreement that allowed Dell to sell Cisco gear on its Web site.

Printers are another adjacent market for which Dell has big growth plans. Hewlett-Packard got so nervous about rumors of Dell's intent that it cancelled Dell as a reseller of its equipment in July 2002. That move simply accelerated Dell's plans. By September, Dell and Lexmark were announcing a joint agreement, with plans for Dell-branded machines in early 2003. In the meantime, Dell channeled its big Christmas volume of consumer demand to Lexmark. By entering the printer fray, Dell can score points in two ways. First, it hopes to gain a big share of a market that earns fat margins from ink cartridges. Second, it plans to dry up Hewlett-Packard's biggest cash cow, where HP holds greater than a 50 percent market share.

Dell's victories in servers, storage, and networks are the underpinning of its computer services sales, now a $3.2 billion business for Dell, that is growing at better than 35 percent annually. But isn't service a deviation from Dell's low-cost, highly automated business model? Not the way Dell is pursuing it. It is avoiding the complex service segments, such as applications development or enterprise software integrations, until they commoditize, and concentrating on more structured infrastructure services, such as operating systems upgrades, conversions, and network expansions.

In each adjacent product market, Dell will leverage its expertise in manufacturing and marketing to deliver the kind of high-volume, out-of-the-box operation that made it dominant in personal computers. It will start at the low end of each market, then move on to faster, more expensive machines as the technology ripens.

To support its adjacent-market strategy, Dell is, for the first time in its history, making acquisitions, such as its purchase of Plural (a two-hundred-person software services company that specializes in Microsoft technologies) in May 2002. These purchases, Rollins said, will be of small, tuck-in companies that can complement Dell's seven-thousand-person-strong services group.

Together, these adjacent markets already account for 20 percent of Dell's revenues, and that is expected to climb to 50 percent by 2007. In the long run, according to Michael Dell, "Servers, storage, and related services are big expansion areas [for us]. I'm as convinced as I've ever been that we'll lead in these enterprises worldwide. It's just a matter of time."

New Lines of Business. In this fifth discipline, Dell Computer has little to show, and that suits Michael Dell just fine. He distrusts any strategic move that diverges from the organization's basic strengths; he still winces at the mistake in the early 1990s that led Dell away from its direct-sales model and into sales in retail outlets, including Staples and CompUSA. At 10 percent of sales, that operation was the fastest-growing part of the business. But it was losing money, and, according to Rollins, "Our analysis said that not only was the business itself bad, but even if we did everything else right it would still be bad." Dell bailed out.

Looking back, Michael Dell considers that misadventure "both a violation of our core business strategy and incredibly confusing to our organization." Yet he adds, "What's interesting is that when we corrected it, there was almost a galvanizing force on the culture and on the strategy of the company. It became crystal clear to everyone what the strategy was and how we're going to execute [it], and it was reinforced with great success and growth."

And that, he has suggested, shows the value of holding fast to what you do best. "At the time, the conventional wisdom was that our company would be relegated to a niche," Dell said. "In fact, one of the things that benefited our growth is that our competitors actually believed that. But fortunately the niche became the whole market. So our focus on executing the business model after that misadventure turned out to be a powerful force for us."

That is precisely Dell's formula for the future: turn a niche into a market, outclass all competitors, and then execute, execute, execute. Its ability to gobble market share has forced every other computer maker to define its strategy in relation—and mostly in reaction—to Dell. It has become the eight-hundred-pound armadillo of the personal-computer world. Michael Dell may be overlooking something in his analysis of his company's future, but, given his track record, it seems unwise to bet against him.

Growth by Disciplines

As we have seen, each of these six companies is unfettered by the operational capacity of any single operating unit. They have grown by finding opportunities beyond the limits of any single market. They all grew by recognizing and seizing opportunities using five specific growth disciplines.

Each company chose a different mix of the five, adjusting its portfolio to its markets, its own capabilities, and its individual situation. But all six enterprises were careful to enforce the first discipline by retaining their base customers; the second discipline by being feisty competitors that took share from their rivals; the third discipline by choosing to position themselves in market segments that were growing faster than the market as a whole; and the fourth discipline by being adept at expanding into adjacent markets. Also, in varying degrees, they proceeded with extreme caution into new lines of business.

The chapters ahead will show you how your business can do as well as these six, and how you can achieve consistent annual double-digit growth by carefully applying the five disciplines. But first, we have to answer the fundamental question: What precisely is growth? In other words, what will managers be measuring?

How Should You Measure Growth?

Blessings (and calories) need counting. Euros need dollars. Electricity needs kilowatts. Music needs notes. Students need grades. You can't play tennis without a net. Measure for measure, we exist because we add and subtract and believe in the bottom line.

What is my yardstick for growth?

Revenue and net profit growth are useful measures, but, in my view, they work best as a supplement to another number—gross profits—that is, revenues minus the direct cost of the goods or services being sold. Gross profits are a direct measure of the value that a company creates for its customers. Subtract from revenue all the costs of raw materials, labor, and other production costs, and what you have is a measure of the value that a company has added to the product above and beyond its material and labor content.

For example, a bag full of groceries worth $20 might contain $4 worth of value produced by the grocer, who stocked shelves and made purchasing convenient. The other $16 goes to the suppliers who produced the contents of the bag. But, you might be willing to pay $100 for those same supplies if they were served to you as a delicious dinner for two in an elegant restaurant. In this case, say the restaurateur has another $44 of direct costs in producing the meal—chefs' and waiters' salaries plus additional supplies. That gives the restaurant a gross profit of $40, ten times that of the grocery store. By paying $100 for the meal, but only $20 for the bag of groceries, you are demonstrating that the restaurant adds ten times as much value to a meal as the grocer. That's the true measure of market size, and a gain in gross profits is the truest measure of growth.

Gross profit numbers eliminate whatever costs and benefits the customer doesn't consider relevant. And, in that light, the annual increase or decrease in a company's gross profit is the best gauge for managers to use internally in determining how their companies are faring and growing in their markets.

I once sat on the board of Prosource Food Distribution, which is now a part of Wal-Mart's McLane distribution business. Prosource had $5 billion in annual sales of food, which we bought from processors and delivered to fast-food and casual-dining restaurants. The combination of its high volume and limited variety of food made it a very efficient business.

Importantly, it felt much smaller than a $5 billion company. All we did was buy the goods for $4.7 billion a year, truck them to our warehouse, and pass them through to the restaurants with a minimum of processing and repackaging. The value we added was real, but relatively small; had we used our revenues to gauge our size, we would have been fooling ourselves. Prosource's markup on a $20 case of food was about $1.20—the value that the customer placed on having it delivered. That number—our gross profit—was, to my mind, the true measure of the company and, by extension, the real yardstick of its growth.

3

First Data Masters
the Disciplines of Growth

I have made the claim that any business can grow at a steady double-digit pace, and I have cited perhaps a dozen companies to back up the point, and maybe at this point you believe this might be possible after all. But how does it actually happen? How do people create and manage a portfolio of strategies in the five disciplines needed for double-digit growth? What really goes on where the rubber meets the road?

None of it is easy. If it were, a lot more companies would be chalking up numbers like Mohawk Industries, Paychex, Johnson Controls, Biomet, Oshkosh Truck, or Dell. But for an object lesson in managing a growth portfolio, we're going to take an up-close-and-personal look at another hugely successful company, First Data Corporation, and the way its chairman and CEO, Charlie Fote (pronounced foe-tea), revolutionized its growth portfolio over the course of a year.

First Data is hardly a household name. Nonetheless, it's a $7.6 billion company, based in Denver, with operations in more than 195 countries and territories around the world. Almost surely, it has touched your life in the past year. First Data processes the largest share of all credit card transactions in the United States and sends out about one third of all credit card statements on behalf of card issuers. Perhaps you're more familiar with its big money transfer business, Western Union, which has been moving money for customers since 1871.

The company was founded in 1992 when American Express decided to convert an expense on its books into a going business, and spun off its credit card processing operations as an independent company. First Data is now three separate, related businesses: Card Issuing Services, which authorizes credit, debit, and retail cards, processes transactions, and bills customers for card issuers, including banks and major retailers; Merchant Services, which handles credit, debit, and check processing services for merchants; and Payment Services, which performs money transfers mainly under the Western Union brand name and offers stored value products, official checks, and money orders. A smaller fourth division, Emerging Payments, was formed a few years ago to identify, invest in, and manage next-generation payment businesses.

First Data has succeeded brilliantly in at least one discipline of growth, positioning itself in markets where fast growth is already happening. Electronic transactions mushroomed to 32 percent of all U.S. payments by 2000, and *The Nilson Report* projects that this figure will rise to 65 percent by 2010. In its first decade as an independent company, First Data chalked up a 500 percent increase in revenues and multiplied its net income sevenfold. That caught Wall Street's attention, and investors bid up First Data's market capitalization eightfold.

But there was a worm nestled deep in this rose. From 1997 to 2000, net income had climbed at a compound annual rate of 38 percent—but that increase masked an anemic annual growth of only 3 percent in total revenues and 4 percent in gross profit. The growth in net income reflected laudable gains in efficiency and productivity, but they couldn't continue indefinitely. Charlie Fote, then chief operating officer, spent most of 2001 wrestling with this problem. He decided to transform First Data's long-term growth strategy and trajectory. But he also decreed that there was no sense in waiting; there must be immediate short-term improvement in the current year's growth.

The methodology Fote used for turning around First Data's portfolio can be a model for any company having growth challenges. Naturally, the details will vary from one company to the next; and, as we'll see, the conditions in a market—mainly its rate of growth and extent of normal customer churning—will play a large part in determining a company's portfolio of growth strategies. But Fote's methodology, beginning with his evaluation and analysis of his company and proceeding through planning and implementation, can be adapted to rescue any company in a similar plight.

The Data on First Data

While First Data was a model of operational excellence in most of its businesses, Fote knew that he had to understand both its strengths and its weaknesses to solve the growth problem.

The strengths were obvious. First, the company was built on an extraordinary infrastructure, with more than three hundred million card accounts in its master file and operations firmly established around the globe. First Data knew the meaning of flawless execution: in 2001, it processed more than ten billion point-of-sale transactions and 109 million money transfers, each of them important to the people involved, with reliability that far surpassed Six Sigma. And it understood that its business was driven by customer convenience. At the end of 2001, First Data was processing card payments in 2.8 million merchant locations around the world. The money transfer business had 120,000 locations—more than twice as many outlets for customers as were offered by McDonald's, Burger King, Starbucks, Wal-Mart, and Kmart, combined.

But First Data's weaknesses were implicit in its strengths.

Because it was so focused on operations, the company had little attention left for innovation. Over the years, it had committed a good deal of capital to new product and new business innovation, but the results were usually less than successful. The company was far better at acquiring a $20 million business and growing it to large scale than it was at germinating an idea and nurturing it to the $20 million level.

First Data was also far better at playing defense than at trying to score. Serving roughly half of all retailers' card needs and holding the largest share of the worldwide money transfer market, the company was the big dog in its industry. Understandably, it spent more time fending off intruders than pushing into new territory and seeking new growth.

Fote also recognized that First Data lacked the full complement of talented people it would need for double-digit growth. Since the company had few hard assets apart from technology and the innovative products that its card-issuing customers were pushing into the market, talent would have to be the prime driver of growth. But like the company as a whole, his people were focused on operations and defense. Fote realized that he would have to grow and recruit a reservoir of talent if First Data were to manage an ever-expanding and more complex set of payments businesses.

The Methodology at First Data

With that clear-eyed appraisal firmly in mind, Fote began charting a strategy for moving First Data onto a growth trajectory. And here he used the four-point methodology that is essential in developing any double-digit growth portfolio:

• *Priority:* Make growth through innovation the top priority for every manager in the organization. Help them all understand that they are responsible for growth. Remember that most management teams have a capacity to focus on no more than three priorities, and current operating performance will always be one of these three. If double-digit growth is ever to happen, it must be one of the other two.

• *Perspective:* Start looking at your business through the lens of the growth portfolio. That means you must measure performance for the past five years in each of the five growth disciplines, and set stretch objectives for growth in each of them. Most management teams don't really understand their growth history. When you look at it with the five disciplines of growth as your lens, you will discover basic truths about past performance, your company's strengths and weaknesses, and where to focus energy for growth.

• *People:* To increase your managers' capacity to grow, make significant investments in internal development and targeted recruiting. This will be the deciding factor in the success or failure of double-digit growth. Accelerating growth adds to the demands on management, and most management teams won't be able to grow at a double-digit pace unless they are reinforced with coaching and fresh, talented blood.

• *Plans:* Build growth plans for each of your business units that will prepare them to exceed the stretch objectives you have already set. Each unit's plan will balance its growth portfolio in a different way to fit the realities of its individual market.

In the end, Fote's approach worked. Through many people's efforts, First Data managed to grow revenues by 13 percent in 2001 and gross profit by 18 percent, up from 4 and 10 percent, respectively, the year prior. They did this despite a difficult economic environment toward the end of the year. The growth in gross profit, a direct measure of the added value the company created for its customers, was perhaps the most gratifying result. At the start of 2002, Fote announced to Wall Street that the long-term growth objective for the organization had been raised to 14 to 17 percent. Privately, he harbored even greater growth ambitions. When First Data closed the books on 2002, results came in right on target with a 15 percent gain in revenues and a 24 percent rise in profits.

Now let's take a much closer look at how it was done.

How Markets Move Portfolios

The first imperative for Fote and his managers was to reach a thorough understanding of the several markets that First Data's three main divisions occupied. Inevitably, a growth portfolio must be tailored to the realities of the market being served; it must emphasize the disciplines that are important in that market. Just as stock traders know that it's foolish to argue with the tape—that is, to buy into a plunging market or sell while prices are booming—business leaders must recognize that they will not be rewarded for overweighting a discipline that's not important in their market.

There are two features of any market that tend to dictate how the growth portfolio will be balanced. The first is the market's underlying growth rate; the second is the rate of churn—the rate at which customers switch from one supplier to another.

The effects of market growth and market churn are sharpest at the extremes: very fast growth or decline; a very high rate of churn or almost none at all. Moderately growing markets or moderately churning markets don't seem to have much effect on the balance of the growth portfolio. In moderate conditions, management teams have many options in constructing a growth portfolio.

As growth or churn slows or increases, however, it forces ever-sharper alternative choices in the portfolio. Historical patterns of growth and churn for a business also help explain how managers have adapted to exploit their particular market. Much as Olympic athletes create muscle mass that is specific to their events, so companies shape their capabilities to match their market demands.

How Fast-Growing Markets Affect Portfolios

First Data's Payment Services division was in a market primarily characterized by its fast growth. Such markets are created when more people are crowding into the market and buying more of whatever is being offered.

Sometimes this comes about purely because of demographic changes. For fifty years, the wave of baby boomers has forced markets to grow simply because there are more people to be served than there were in the prior generation. Similarly, the regional population boom in the desert Southwest of the United States has fueled a twenty-year expansion in home building, auto sales, and other industries that prosper with household formation.

At other times, markets grow because there has been a significant leap in the customer value they offer. Usually that's driven either by a technology breakthrough (think Internet shopping or cell phones) or by a business-model innovation (deep-discount airlines or big-box stores).

In the case of First Data's Payment Services, fast growth has been mainly due to demographics. Western Union, the largest of the Payment Services businesses, is in a market fueled by economic migration from poor to rich countries, which generates demand to send money back home. As rich countries get richer and poor countries stay poor, this form of money transfer grows and grows. In most markets around the world, fast and reliable money transfer didn't exist before Western Union came along. In many markets it remains this way today, with Western Union maintaining a significant majority of the money transfer market share originating from the United States, according to *The Nilson Report.* Globally, the division accounts for a smaller share of all consumer money transfers, but the majority of transfers when money's needed very quickly and reliably.

Payment Services' second major business, commercial bill payments, is fueled by an economic trend, the growth in slow-to-pay or delinquent consumer debt. And the division's third business, processing official checks and money orders for financial institutions, has grown steadily with the expansion and increasing complexity of the financial markets. The final business, topping up prepaid cards and mobile phone accounts, is showing great prospects for international growth.

How does a fast-growing market help shape a company's growth portfolio? By definition, an enterprise can grow substantially in this market just by maintaining its market share. Thus its biggest impact on the growth strategy is that *market positioning* becomes the dominant discipline in the portfolio. Since a market has many segments that may show markedly different growth rates, market positioning means picking the right segments and doing everything necessary to get your fair share of them.

But fast-growing markets usually offer little reason to look for *adjacent growth* opportunities, let alone to go into a new and unrelated line of business, since the core market is providing more than enough opportunity. Why fish in unknown water when there are plenty of fish in your own pond?

But remember, no market can sustain high growth rates indefinitely. The trick is to win this phase of market expansion and position yourself for a graceful transition when the market growth rate inevitably slows. *Share gain* is therefore another important discipline in a fast-growing market.

On the face of it, this might seem unnecessary. Since there's more growth in the market's core than most competitors can handle, a company would seem to have little interest in snaring customers beyond the core. But when the market begins to mature and the growth slows down, it's a game of musical chairs. The organization that has built the deepest base of customers and the broadest base of markets wins, and the rest fall by the wayside. Remember Sega? It failed to stay with the lead pack in electronic gaming hardware and had to leave the business. Palm, the maker of the Pilot personal data assistant, is on the cusp of irrelevancy in the industry it actually pioneered. Organically driven share gain must be an important part of any organization's growth strategy in a fast-growing market.

Competitors often fight hard for customer value leadership in fast-growing markets, driving values to higher and higher levels. Success brings added market share, but lagging behind means that the enterprise will almost certainly falter and fail. Maintaining equilibrium, neither growing nor losing market share, is not a viable option.

Surprisingly, this intense focus on customer value tends to reduce the emphasis on *base retention*. Consider the wireless industry during its heady recent growth. Customers were routinely treated to better coverage and sharper prices—but the competing companies, stressed by the costs of the race, routinely "milked" their base of existing customers by offering better value only to new customers. The result? Customers had to switch suppliers to get better value, and they didn't hesitate as soon as they found out what was available. So the companies wound up in an expensive game of trading customers. Meanwhile, other value features—accurate billing, high-touch customer service, service feature innovation—got far less attention as the main battle was being fought over coverage and price. Thus, in a market with exploding levels of value, many customers paradoxically felt underserved and disgruntled.

Typical high-growth markets seldom see share gain through *acquisitions*. This is because everything is too expensive to buy. Since all the competitors think they have a shot at winning the game, no one accepts reasonable valuations. In addition, managers typically think they don't have the capacity to deal with integrating their acquisitions. All that said, however, it can be a tactical mistake to neglect acquisitions in fast-growing markets. In the footrace for leadership, a merger with a promising company can leapfrog your market share and take competitors out of play.

How Flat Markets Affect Portfolios

As we all know, however, not all markets are fast-growing. Some markets stagnate; others shrink. First Data's Card Issuing Services division, which had operated for years in a high-growth market, found itself first in stagnation and then in outright decline. In such markets, total gross profits earned by the industry dwindle, even if revenues remain constant. Sometimes these markets shrink to the vanishing point; they are going out of business as they are replaced by other markets.

First Data's Card Issuing Services division is typical of a market leader in a flat market. Its business is providing outsourcing services for credit, debit, and private-label card issuers. It embosses plastics, mails cards and statements, and provides the back-office processing services for fourteen hundred card issuers and more than three hundred million accounts. For many years, the industry showed healthy growth as people carried more and more plastic in their wallets, and the Card Issuing Services division grew to service almost one third of all that plastic. But the market is now saturated, growing very slowly, and hurt by high default rates in the formerly profitable high-risk market segment.

The result has been a steady decline in total industry gross profits as new card issuance slows and issuers consolidate. As with many other things in life, the pain is transferred, in this case to the issuers' supplier, Card Issuing Services. Bad day at the office? Go home and yell at the dog. A problem growing profits in your card business? Squeeze the suppliers for every penny they've got. In 2001, Card Issuing Services chalked up less than 2 percent growth in revenue, almost all of it through acquisitions. It took some very diligent work just to keep gross profits at year-earlier levels.

Some businesses decline because they are victims of technology. The industry that makes paper-based diaries, organizers, and calendars, for instance, is dwindling as its products are replaced by electronic personal digital assistant devices. The traditional toy market, too, has been in decline for several years. It's not going out of business, but demand has been siphoned off by the electronic game producers dominated by Nintendo, Microsoft, EA Software, and other high-tech companies.

Markets decline for reasons diametrically opposed to the reasons why other markets grow. Basically, the value that the declining market delivers is trumped by better value in another market, so that people either buy less or leave the market altogether. In these conditions, gross margin and profits dry up long before revenues (unless there is a high-margin maintenance annuity in the market, as there is in the software industry). Thus, in many of these markets, revenue may still be growing modestly. But the customers no longer value the product or service as they once did, and the industry isn't coming up with enough innovation to counteract the march to commoditization.

The most obvious effect of a declining market in shaping the growth portfolio is that a company will find growth almost impossible in its core market. Beyond that, since profit margins are shrinking, there is little incentive to steal customers away from competitors. Thus, *base retention* becomes a major element of the growth portfolio. The game is to lose less than your fair share as the market contracts. Often, this effort so preoccupies managers that they have little time for the more important issue of what to do when the market has fully declined. Domestic airlines, for instance, have been in decline for many years, and they were among the first to invest in elaborate base retention programs. In fact, their frequent flyer programs have been the model for many other industries in shrinking markets.

The other major element of a growth portfolio in a declining market is *share gain*, not by stealing customers but through acquisitions. The goal is to create scale economies and squeeze out costs. In effect, the decline in gross profits forces the industry to consolidate to find efficiencies and gain more bargaining power against increasingly aggressive customers. Acquisitions can be particularly attractive in a declining market because valuations are low and affordable. Retail banking, for example, has been in decline as profitable businesses have been stripped away from banks by specialized competitors in credit cards, home mortgages, auto finance, and investments. The industry has responded by consolidating. It is God's way of recycling bankers into more productive roles.

Market positioning is usually important in a declining market, but only in the early stages. Not all segments of a market decline at the same pace, but in most cases they all reach the same destination—wrack and ruin. A few years back in the domestic airline business, it was fashionable to talk about the positional advantage of United and American Airlines. The theory was that their main market segment—long-haul routes—made them less vulnerable than other major airlines to deep-discount, short-haul carriers such as Southwest Airlines, and that their major hubs in the center of the country gave them advantages for east–west traffic. That worked out for a while, but where are they now? Eventually, all segments of a declining market will regress to a low mean.

Surprisingly, there is less focus on *adjacent growth* in a declining market than you might expect. Given that the ship is sinking, you would think that all hands would be on deck to find new vessels to jump to, but often this isn't the case. Why? Probably because management is too preoccupied by the sinking ship, mistakenly thinking that it can be kept afloat. But there's another reason, too. Often, the ship is sinking because the management fell behind in all three critical capabilities: technology, market understanding, and business model. If that's the case, what leverage could the company bring to adjacent markets?

How Market Churn Rate Affects Portfolios

After the underlying growth rate, the second major market factor that affects portfolio strategy is the rate of customer churning. And on this point, the first thing we have to do is clear up a major fallacy.

There is a common assumption about churning: that some customers are inherently more loyal to their suppliers than others. It follows logically that if you can simply find and capture the loyal customers, you'll automatically have a better business.

The trouble with this is that no customers are loyal to any suppliers. Customers are loyal to only one thing—best value. If customers can find better value in another supplier, they will take their business there. If customers can't find or don't know about better value elsewhere, they stay with the supplier they have. So whether an industry experiences high churn depends not on the inherent characteristics of its customers, but on the pace and source of customer value improvement. Does loyalty management have anything to add to this discussion? Not where I come from.

In low-churn or moderate-churn markets, like the one occupied by First Data's Merchant Services division, it is hard for customers to find better value than what they are already getting. Why is this so difficult? It's usually one of three factors.

The first occurs when all the competitors offer pretty much the same thing, so there aren't sharp differences in the values of their offerings. That's the case in retail banking. Try as you might, it's hard to find a bank that has a really distinctive and attractive offer. They all meet just about the same minimal standards of service, cost, and product innovation.

The second factor comes into play when the customer searches in a narrow range of alternatives, so that even if there is truly better value out there, the customer isn't looking widely enough to find it. This is the case in life insurance. There is a bewildering array of features offered in life insurance policies, and some offerings are much better than others. What's missing is any inclination on the part of the average customer to wade through all the mumbo jumbo and actually find the best value. That's why most of us narrow our range of choice to insurance agents, many of whom are optimizing their take on the deal, not value for us.

The third factor that can create a low-churn market is switching costs. If I offer you half price on your telephone service forever, that's a great deal. But if you have to rewire your house to get it, it may not be so attractive after all. To a homeowner who plans to live in the house for a long time, perhaps it's worth it, but to most others, the long-term savings won't outweigh the one-time cost.

Switching costs are everywhere, and they're not always monetary. Familiarity creates switching costs. I know where all the stations are on my cable system. It will cost me time and effort to relearn them on a satellite system. (That, apparently, is a switching cost that more and more people are willing to pay.) My investment advisor has learned a lot about how I want to invest. Even if the guy has given me a lot of bad advice, do I really have the time and patience to break in someone new? Never underestimate switching costs. They've kept bad value in circulation in a lot of markets for a long time.

Businesses in low-churn markets include:

• Full-service investment management. All the competitors offer roughly the same quality of service at about the same rates, and the switching cost of training a new advisor is huge. Interestingly, however, in self-directed investment services (think Fidelity, Schwab, and Vanguard), there are some real differences in value propositions and the switching costs are substantially lower than in full-service brokerages. In fact, the value propositions of Fidelity, Schwab, and Vanguard are so powerful that they are successfully stealing away market share from the full-service investment management firms at a prodigious clip.

• Insurance. It's complicated; it's not fun; it's hard to get information. So, I'll let my agent do the work and pray that he doesn't take me for a ride. Should I be nervous that he's always treating me to a game of golf?

• Industrial suppliers of custom products. For example, take chemical producers that supply custom formulated plastics to a particular manufacturer. In these instances, the customer is entering into a sole-supplier relationship to give the supplier an incentive to invest time, energy, and money in the development of a custom product. Very high switching costs keep the customers in place because they usually can't ask others to supply the customized product.

• Outsourcing industries, including payroll services, computer out-sourcing, and administrative outsourcing. Once the outsourcing orga-nization has taken over the job and you have given up your ability to do it yourself, where are you going to go? Even if there's another sup-plier available, it will take a huge effort to integrate the new one in your operation. The switching cost has become almost infinite.

The Merchant Services division is, in effect, two large businesses: First Data Merchant Services, offering the services and equipment to accept and redeem credit and debit card payments at three million point-of-sale mercant locations, and TeleCheck, which guarantees more than 3.4 billion checks used to pay for goods worth $171 billion a year at 210,000 different retail locations. TeleCheck's latest technol-ogy instantly turns a paper check, written at a checkout counter, into an electronic payment by automatically debiting the bank account on which the check is drawn. It's bringing checking into the modern age.

First Data's Merchant Services has been able to grow its revenues at a rate of more than 15 percent for the past several years, and most of that growth has come through acquisitions. First Data has found that acquisitions are more cost-effective than going door to door and sell-ing merchant contracts one at a time. Its strategy has been to persuade banks with merchant servicing operations to sell First Data a portion of their business, including all the back-end processing, which leaves the banks free to focus their own efforts on growing their base of lo-cal and regional retailers using the service. The effect has been that First Data has captured a large share of the market while still giving its partners incentive to grow market share. It is a particularly creative and effective strategy.

If you are in a low-churn market and can count on your customer base being there year in and year out, how does that fact shape the balance of disciplines in your growth portfolio?

Share gain through in-line acquisitions will probably be a major part of your growth strategy. As Merchant Services has found, it's often cheaper in a low-churn market to buy a company's customer base than to gain share organically, one client at a time.

Entering *adjacent markets,* where new products and services can be sold to existing customers, is another key discipline in a low-churn growth portfolio. Relationships are a major asset for businesses in these markets.

That said, many organizations stumble in adjacent markets because they don't know the difference between cross-selling and cross-purchasing. In cross-selling, the supplier is trying to push additional products and services onto its existing customer base. Such enterprises often assume that their relationships are so strong that they can persuade customers to accept adjacent offerings that are no better than average in value. This fails to reckon with switching costs, which might be too high for an average offering to overcome. In true cross-buying, the supplier starts from the customer's perspective, trying to see how the combination of the supplier's core offering with an adjacent product will give the client added value.

Base retention is a minor part of the low-churn growth portfolio, even though it contributes a lot to overall growth. In high-retention industries, there's no reason to spend more than a little time and energy trying to improve what's already excellent. The return on further investment would be negligible.

Whether churning is high or low, it has little impact on *market positioning* as a discipline in the growth portfolio. As a practical matter, your positioning strategy is not affected by the churn rate.

There are also markets with a high rate of customer churning. In these markets, it is relatively easy for customers to find better value than they are getting. The same three basic factors are at work as in low-churn markets, but in reverse.

First, the industry offers rapid improvement in value. In fact, there's something of a customer-value arms race under way. As we saw in the telecom industry, companies fighting for new customers offer their best deals to newcomers, leaving their current customers to be picked off by competitors. This isn't as stupid as it may seem. The suppliers are banking on customer lethargy. In telecommunications and high-tech industries, for instance, the latest product is always cheaper or functionally better than older offerings, but most users won't replace their systems every year. The long-distance industry offers better value on almost a monthly basis, but no customer will go through the stress of changing service suppliers anything like that often.

The second factor in making it easy to find better value is widening the range of choice, and in high-churn markets, customers are bombarded with hundred-decibel advertising to alert them to the opportunity for better value. The customer is goaded into looking at a wide range of alternatives. Who could overcome the guilt of being too lazy to search out a better deal on a new car?

The third factor in finding better value is switching costs, and some industries in high-churn markets have made it almost effortless to switch suppliers. Of course, this has left the gate open for competitors to steal their customers in return. Consider the airline industry. Flying from Chicago, you almost always have at least two choices: American and United. If you arrive at the airport a little early for your flight, it is no problem to check whether the other airline has an earlier flight. And if you want to switch, that's no problem either. Call your new choice by cell phone to ensure availability and simply show up at the gate with the competitor's ticket. Hungry for revenue, they'll take it, even if it's deeply discounted, because after all, anything is better than taking off with an empty seat.

In high-churn markets, an annual loss of more than 20 percent of an organization's customers is the norm. Therefore, at least that much growth must be found somewhere in the portfolio just to prevent shrinkage.

Besides airlines, telecommunications, and high tech, industries in high-churn markets include:

- Any commodity product. By definition, a commodity is something with near-zero switching cost, and customers can be motivated to switch with only small improvements in value.
- Surprisingly, automobiles. The best brands see only 30 percent of their customers return for a repeat purchase.

If you are in a high-churn market and you know that every one of your customers is ready to jump to the next best deal that comes along, what do you do? How does that fact shape your growth portfolio?

Base retention must be a major part of the portfolio of a company in a high-churn market. If the organization can lose customers more slowly than its competitors, it will score the best overall growth. This is obvious, but even so, companies that compete in low-retention industries tend to neglect their base retention—probably because they are so aggressively focused on attracting replacement customers. No matter how many times the message is delivered about the advantage of retaining the ones they've got, it never seems to sink in.

Share gain through organic means must also be a major part of such a company's growth strategy. With high churn, its competitors' customers are always open to the right offer. In some high-churn markets, as many as half the customers change suppliers each year. What attracts those customers is just one thing: best value. But shout it loud and clear. If you want to build market share, your company must make sure potential customers are aware of your superior proposition.

Entering *adjacent markets* may be an important discipline in the high-churn growth portfolio, usually employed out of desperate necessity. Rarely can a corporation leverage existing customer relationships, since those relationships are so fleeting. It must be some other capability, embedded in the business model, that provides the advantage for entry into an adjacent market.

Acquisitions have a unique role in high-churn markets. An acquisition intended for share gain is usually not worth the price, because the customer base you are buying is so ephemeral. At rock-bottom prices there may be the rare opportunity to acquire weaker competitors in order to reduce competitive intensity. This is a war of attrition, in which churn will slow down only when the number of competitors is significantly reduced.

As in low-churn markets, strategies for *market positioning* growth are not affected by market churn rates.

The First Step at First Data—Priorities

Having analyzed First Data's various markets, Fote could now embark on the four-point methodology for achieving double-digit growth. He would set new priorities throughout the company, making growth the number-one objective. He would push his managers to view their operations, past and future, through the lens of the growth portfolio, and set objectives for each unit that would stretch their capacities. He would invest in internal development of his people and use targeted recruiting to raise his management team's capacity for growth. And he would develop growth plans for each of his businesses that would exceed their stretch objectives.

Fote's first step in the four-pronged methodology was to get the company and its managers focused on a new set of priorities, making growth their number-one objective.

He called his forty top executives from around the world to a special meeting at the Denver headquarters. He challenged them to create a First Data that could achieve aggressive growth in revenues, operating profit, and net income. And the challenge started with the current year's results—"Why wait? Do it now!" He made the team feel his own sense of urgency and commitment to the cause. This, they understood, was Charlie's goal and Charlie's priority. Fote has enormous powers of persuasion over his management team because they know he is fully committed to the success of the company. No one works harder; no one cares more for employees and shareholders; no one is more forthright and honest about what's working and what's not. He has earned the respect that any dedicated leader must have in order to win.

To reinforce that message, Fote also put his personal reputation on the line with a public commitment to the goals. In January 2002, in his first meeting with securities analysts as the new CEO of First Data, Fote announced that he was raising his long-term growth expectations to 14 to 17 percent and that he expected to grow earnings per share by 15 to 18 percent in the coming year. This was above anything that the analysts had expected for the company. Fote made these commitments before he had all the ducks in a row for a plan to achieve them. But he also knew that these pronouncements were a way of creating the right heat and pressure on his own management team to dig deep and find ways to make it happen.

Fote took his message of growth inside the organization, as well. In quarterly company updates, broadcast live to the entire corporation, he stressed the importance of growth and discussed the commitment that he had made to Wall Street. Growth became a part of the buzz in his daily interactions with employees at all levels in the organization.

"How are we going to get this business growing even faster than it is today? What ideas do you have?" Before long, everyone understood that this charismatic leader was on a mission and they joined the mission, too.

The Second Step at First Data—Perspective

Starting at the Denver meeting and continuing for months, the top managers worked on the next step in the methodology—understanding First Data's growth history through the lens of the five disciplines in the growth portfolio. Each of the company's three major businesses differed from the others, and, as we have seen, they operated in basically different markets. All of them had benefited from good market positioning, setting up shop in a market that was growing fast—but the individual markets had changed over time. And for First Data, one of the five disciplines of growth would be irrelevant: as a matter of corporate strategy, none of the divisions would go into any new lines of business. The company avoids investing in markets that are not adjacent to its core businesses, reasoning that there's just too much opportunity up close to go fishing far afield.

This view was also tempered by the company's experience in teleservices. It had entered this market several years earlier as an adjacent market to its then-significant telemarketing business—a business they have long since exited. First Data has struggled to find ways to apply its capabilities to this people-intensive business and concluded that teleservices wasn't very related at all to its core capabilities. It remains as a very small part of the company. Fote vowed to avoid this mistake in the future by keeping the divisions focused on opportunities related to their core capabilities.

Let's look at how the growth portfolios of First Data's three divisions shaped up at the end of the assessment process.

Payment Services

The division operates in a robustly growing market. Money transfers have more than doubled in the past five years, with international money transfers growing at more than 30 percent every year. The division's market is made up of thousands of different corridors along which payments travel (U.S. to Somalia, for instance, or Germany to Turkey). Most of its growth has come from *market positioning*—moving into fast-growing market segments and getting at least its fair share, especially in the international money transfer segments. Payment Services has also successfully moved money transfer onto the Internet, where growth has been brisk, but not yet approaching the levels of its brick-and-mortar storefronts.

Base retention is an important discipline in the growth portfolio of the bill payment side of Payment Services, where the clients include large commercial billers, such as Ford Motor Credit. But the company had little insight into base retention in the consumer money transfer business, because its systems were not set up to easily track clients' repeat purchases. Fote and his managers suspected that they could be doing much better at retaining consumer business if they could track the records.

The division has struggled to maintain *market share* as price-aggressive competitors have entered more mature markets, such as the U.S.-to-Mexico corridor. But managers found it hard to calculate the market share of all the informal money transfer arrangements that are set up in immigrant communities. For instance, when the owner of a corner bodega in Spanish Harlem transfers money back to one city in Colombia, where his cousin's gas station is the cash dispensing point, the transaction is nearly invisible.

The major *market adjacency* that Payment Services has exploited—leveraging its money transfer business into the commercial bill payment market—was started more than ten years ago, and has been a major success. From twenty-five thousand transactions the first year, the business has grown to produce triple that number *each day*. Since then, the division has exploited several segments within the commercial market. In 2002, for instance, Payment Services acquired Paymap, a company that offers electronic payment technology to the mortgage industry. A year earlier it acquired BidPay to compete with PayPal in the Internet person-to-person payment market. These adjacencies have done well. Although they initially added less than 2 percent to the overall revenue of the company, together they are growing at a very fast clip.

Reevaluating the division's growth history caused its managers to realize just how much of their growth was created by wisely positioning the division in rapidly expanding markets. Their efforts to reposition the organization from domestic to international money transfer and to put themselves in the Internet channel have paid off with outstanding growth results. In addition, the innovative application of their money transfer capabilities in the commercial bill payment market created another major growth success. Were there similar adjacencies yet to be discovered?

The managers were also forced to reexamine their efforts in money transfer corridors where growth was slowing. Here, they realized, they needed a different type of management skill and focus to be able to grow market share in the face of insurgent competition.

Finally, the managers were chastened by their inability to track base retention in the division's core business. They realized that to manage growth, they must measure base retention as they go forward.

With the strong underlying growth of the market and a focused strategy, the management team came to conclude that they could substantially raise their growth ambitions for this business. They set a target for domestic transaction growth above 20 percent and committed to grow international transactions at better than 30 percent per year. It would be a stretch, but Charlie Fote and the team thought that these were achievable growth goals.

Merchant Services

In the previous three years before Fote's assessment, this division had almost doubled its growth rate to nearly 20 percent per year, and operating profits had kept pace with this growth. However, operating margins had dropped from 24 percent to 15 percent over the same period—an aberration, Fote and his managers concluded, caused by the cost of integrating some large acquisitions.

The growth of Merchant Services had come mainly from growing *market share* through its alliance strategy, devised some years ago, of buying portions of the merchant servicing operations of banks and taking over the back-end processing. The banks kept expanding the business by growing their bases of local and regional retailers using the service, and Merchant Services reaped significant cost savings by converting the acquisitions to their own processing platforms. The decision to gain market share through acquisitions rather than through organic growth was simply sound economics. As we have seen, it is less expensive to acquire customers in low-churn markets by acquiring similar businesses than by organic growth.

The division had exploited one *market adjacency* with the acquisition of TASQ in point-of-sale equipment. TASQ is a $92 million supplier of all the hardware, software, and related services that a merchant needs to accept and redeem credit and debit card payments. It sells its services through banks' merchant servicing operations so that the banks can provide turnkey services to retailers without having to invest in highly specialized capabilities. This adjacent acquisition was a natural for Merchant Services, given its highly successful bank alliances. Merchant Services had benefited from strong *base retention.* Most of its business is done under multiyear contracts, and the costs of switching to competing suppliers are relatively high. And unlike the situation in the Card Issuing division, there is little incentive for customers to take their processing back in-house.

Market positioning had been strong in the core business. Point-of-sale credit card transactions had increased from 5.3 billion to 10.1 billion in the previous five years. In other areas, however, Merchant Services had failed to exploit opportunities. The division was slow to grow into international markets, and has remained mainly a U.S.-based business. It also failed to predict the rapid rise of debit card usage and was number two in that market, an unfamiliar position. To bolster its position in debit card processing, in August 2001, First Data acquired a majority interest in NYCE, an ATM network that allows transactions to be debited and credited directly against bank accounts. ATMs are the processing backbone for the fast-growing debit card market and this acquisition allowed Merchant Services to make up some ground in this important market segment.

Putting the division under the growth spotlight changed its managers' perspective on their past successes. It highlighted the success of the bank alliance strategy, but also how dependent the division had been on acquisitions for growth. Overall, more than two thirds of Merchant Services' growth had come through bank alliance consolidations. The dependence on acquisitions also raised some issues of balance. Did this division have the capacity to grow faster through organic means? Could it increase market share on its own, even if that would be a more expensive way to acquire customers? Could the division create adjacent growth that would be based on internal innovation, or must it always use its checkbook to acquire a base business from which it could expand? Also considered were the division's strength and weakness in various vertical market segments, such as petroleum retailing and department stores. Could the company become uniformly strong across all vertical market segments?

Unlike the Payment Services division, Merchant Services could not count on robust underlying market growth to "float its boat." There was still growth to be had in further bank alliances, but additional sources of growth needed to be found. It would be a big accomplishment to get this division to grow at 20-plus percent per year, but that would be the target.

Card Issuing Services

Revenue in the Card Issuing Services business had been flat to declining, and profits were growing only by wringing out costs every year. These dismal figures were due primarily to adverse market positioning: the early fast growth in the card market had dried up, and the industry itself was consolidating. Base retention and market share gain had been neutral. Adjacent expansion had been largely unexplored.

Market positioning—sitting on top of a fast-growing market and getting fair share—had been the division's basic approach to growth for many years. More and more consumers were carrying more and more plastic, and the division's revenue was primarily driven by the total number of cards outstanding, not by how often they were used. From 1995 to 1999, cards on file grew at a pace of nearly 20 percent per year. But that trend was over—by 2001, it seemed that everyone in the United States had more than enough plastic. Suddenly the choice of market segments—international versus domestic, bank card versus retail card—had become very important, and the division wasn't positioned in the faster-growing international segments.

Base retention had been hit hard by the consolidation of the banking business. Fewer and fewer financial institutions remained in the maturing card-issuing industry. This gave customers greater bargaining power, which undermined gross and net profits. With each consolidation, another client used the opportunity to re-open long-term contracts and drive tougher and tougher terms. Even when Card Issuing Services could keep the consolidated clients, it was hard to keep the same gross margin.

Market share was being measured in larger and larger chunks as demand consolidated in the hands of ever-fewer financial institutions. Since the business was done in multiyear contracts with high switching costs, gaining new business from large credit card issuers was difficult and expensive. The real battle for market share was between insourced and outsourced operations. The Card Issuing Services division originally offered economies of scale as an outsourcer, but the pendulum was swinging back toward insourcing, since the largest players now had the scale to reach full operational efficiency.

The division was providing a wide array of services for credit card issuers on an *à la carte* menu. It had not explored *market adjacencies* that would complement and leverage these offerings, and there were many such adjacencies. The new lens of growth perspective brought several major issues into focus for the management team.

Market positioning, for openers, had been going sour for several years. But market position is a given only if it isn't actively managed. Why hadn't the division done anything about it? Had the division made matters worse by concentrating on large issuers of cards—the very customers who have maximum leverage on price and gross margin?

This division was processing more than one third of all the credit card accounts in North America. Why hadn't it built a whopping cost advantage that could translate into significant value leadership? With its scale advantages, Card Issuing Services should have been the only enterprise that could put enough value on the table to overcome the huge switching costs of this marketplace. The division should have been taking market share from its competitors at a prodigious rate, and it wasn't. Something was wrong.

Market adjacencies remained largely unexamined. Given the division's dismal growth history, shouldn't this change? And there were lots of adjacencies to examine, up and down the card value chain, from card marketing to collections. The division could also go into adjacent forms of bank process outsourcing, from checking accounts to loan administration. Or it could transform other markets to the card payment model, offering a great deal of added value. The business of Card Issuing Services handles every aspect of a consumer's credit card account—processing the initial application, issuing and reissuing the card, authorization of purchases, fraud detection, issuing monthly statements, and collecting payments from consumers. These basic account processes are performed less efficiently in a host of other markets including frequent flyer airline accounts, healthcare insurance, and telecommunications billing. Why weren't these markets that Card Issuing Services was growing in? Because these opportunities had been left largely unexplored.

The stretch objective for this division needed to be to start growing again. Fote knew he wasn't going to get it to the 20 percent growth target anytime soon, but couldn't it at least reach a double-digit growth level with some success in adjacent markets?

The Third Step at First Data—People

To meet his double-digit growth goals, Fote realized that the whole company must sharply improve its ability to attract, develop, and retain management talent.

Developing talent is a line-management job; it is a core responsibility, not an extracurricular activity. Fote knew that it couldn't be left to the human resources department or the company's organizational development folks. It must be required of every manager, and it must be measured and rewarded.

Two concerted efforts would have the greatest impact. First, high-potential people would get personal coaching, and this would be both formal (training in performance management) and informal (frequent feedback). Then people would be given stretch assignments that would provide the maximum opportunity to develop.

Fote also understood that talent development flows from the top down: people will follow their leaders' examples. Therefore he needed to get all of his senior team committed to increasing the company's capacity to develop talent. He decided to focus on the next generation of First Data's leaders, the two layers below the Executive Committee.

The approach he chose was to address current and desired performance in five elements of people management.

First, there would be a vigorous *recruiting* drive to attract promising talent. Recruiters would be more closely connected to the business, and recent hires, both successful and unsuccessful, would be profiled to provide guidelines for choosing recruits. New hires would be told to expect to move around within the company. And an associates program would be set up to recruit talent at the college and MBA levels.

To *integrate* the newcomers into the company, there would be a formal program that would teach them about First Data, expose them systematically to senior management, and help them build a network across the three divisions. Another management process would periodically evaluate the company's bench strength and identify successes and failures.

Development of talent would be strengthened as a line management responsibility, with performance management as the key tool. People would be given formal training to build their knowledge of First Data and the industry in general and to develop skills in such areas as new product development and developing business models.

Since people were to be regarded as an asset of the whole company, they would be carefully *deployed* to share the wealth. Promising people would get stretch assignments in all three divisions to increase their abilities and build experience, and they would be exposed to opportunities to work across corporate boundaries as well.

To *retain* talented managers, senior executives would mentor them in personal relationships. There would be rewards and recognition for successes, but there would also be a safety net for those in risky assignments. And if talented people left the company despite this opportunity-rich environment, they would explain why in exit interviews that would help First Data avoid future losses.

Fote needed quick results that would have an impact in 2002, so he set up a short-term program to be run by the Executive Committee. The committee chose fifty general management candidates to be functional leaders and gave them development programs that were tailored to their personal needs.

But the emphasis was on broad-based development programs for the long term, and these are only beginning to show any results for First Data. The recruiting effort has been a great improvement, and, despite some disappointments, the integration and bench development processes are beginning to yield results.

Performance management has used both carrots and sticks, leading by example and proceeding from a focus on weak performers to the development of both top players and supporting teams. Skill training has given talented people the tools for success, first at lower levels of the company and then in positions to become its next generation of leaders. And Fote has monitored the program to make sure that the safety nets work and that success is recognized and rewarded with new opportunities, so that talented people won't become frustrated and cynical.

The Fourth Step at First Data—Plans

The final step in the four-pronged growth methodology was to make concrete plans for each business unit, calculated to exceed the stretch growth targets that had been set for them.

CEO Fote realized that his first move must be to clean up the deadwood—to get rid of First Data's chronically underperforming units that had been masking the relatively strong performance of the major business units.

That done, however, the key to the growth strategy would be to build specific plans for each of First Data's three divisions that would equip them to meet and even exceed their stretch objectives. Again, we'll take them in order.

Payment Services

In the money transfer business where First Data's Western Union brand is ubiquitous, growth would continue to be generated mostly from *market positioning*. There was a dramatic difference in the growth rates of different money transfer corridors. Such segments as U.S. to Mexico were mature and growing at single-digit rates. But other corridors, such as Hong Kong to Philippines, U.S. to India, and U.S. to China, were growing very quickly, some at annual rates in the triple digits. Therefore, the key to Western Union's growth strategy was to invest in those segments where the greatest growth would be found.

In practice, this meant seeking out immature markets where competition is scarce. The division must build a global presence, especially in big, emigrant-producing nations with explosive growth potential, such as China, India, and Indonesia. And since the money transfer business is convenience-driven and cash-based, Western Union must have many conveniently located agents in each country.

Since the close of 2000, Western Union has planted the flag in ten new countries and increased its agent locations by 50 percent, to 151,000 worldwide locations at the end of 2002. This location expansion helped enable international transaction growth of 43 percent in 2001 and 32 percent in 2002. Some at the company foresee a future with five or six hundred thousand Western Union locations spread across every corner of the world.

But Western Union had no intention of abandoning the mature markets where competition is growing, so the second element of the Payment Services growth portfolio was *share gain*. To achieve this, Western Union has had to sharpen its value proposition. In the mature market segments, Western Union had traditionally viewed loss of market share as the inevitable price of maintaining high profits. More recently, the division has turned share losses into share gains by sharpening its value proposition—cutting prices and beefing up service—and funding the improvements not through reduced profit margins, but by cost cuts and productivity gains. The improvement in value proposition has been substantial. By one reckoning, Western Union's value pricing in Mexico has improved by as much as 40 percent.

This focus on value proposition began to pay dividends right away. Market share erosion in the U.S.-to-Mexico segment, for example, has turned around. Clients are sticking with Western Union rather than defecting to some other provider, and they are starting to gain market share.

A second way that the division has increased market share is by continuing to expand the agent network. The more locations Western Union has, especially in new regions, the more convenient becomes its service and the more dominating its brand presence. Improved convenience helps retain existing customers as well as attract new ones.

The division is just beginning to focus on *base retention,* with the task of measuring customer retention as a first step. If they can be tracked, repeat customers are both profitable and predictable; they transfer money home on a weekly or monthly cycle. To retain this base of customers, Western Union would sharpen its value proposition, by cutting prices, improving the customer experience provided by the agent, and adding features such as a free phone call for each money transfer.

For customers who send money mainly in emergencies, the occasion for money transfer is by definition unpredictable. Western Union could retain this part of its base only by investing in brand awareness to keep the product at the top of the customer's mind when an emergency comes along.

And Western Union developed aggressive plans to penetrate *adja-*

cent markets. Its managers know that many of its immigrant customers do not have a bank account; even as they climb the economic ladder in their adopted country, they may remain distrustful of large institutions. Yet they have increasingly complex financial needs. Western Union sees this as an opportunity to leverage its familiar brand, its agent network, and its payments know-how into a series of adjacent financial services. It has also identified the burgeoning prepaid card industry, used extensively for mobile phone accounts and other services outside of the United States, as a huge opportunity for adjacent growth. Like money transfer, the business is based on receiving cash and quickly and accurately transferring that value to some other location, in this case, perhaps, a mobile phone account. The management team at Payment Services thinks that the replenishment or "top-up" of prepaid cards may grow to become a major business for them someday. All told, the future looks rosy indeed for this money transfer powerhouse.

Merchant Services

The Merchant Services division operates in a lower-churn marketplace, where, as we've seen, base retention is less of a problem and organic share gain is a bigger challenge. Thus, it plans to increase its growth rates by focusing on growing market share through acquisitions, adjacent expansion, base retention, and market positioning, in that order of priority.

Merchant Services has scored steady *share gain* over the years through a little organic growth and a lot of partial or complete acquisitions in its bank alliance program. Banks in the Merchant Services alliance program include JP Morgan Chase, Fleet, Wachovia, Wells Fargo, and Huntington Bank. Over time, Merchant Services has increased its ownership in several of the alliances, thus acquiring further market share of businesses that are already integrated into its operations.

First Data saw an opportunity in 2002 to further its market share in PIN-based debit cards by acquiring PayPoint from BP p.l.c. That acquisition also strengthened its share in key vertical markets by adding a huge customer base of petroleum, grocery, and fast-food outlets. Overnight, First Data gained the number-one overall position in debit card processing.

The company believes that there are several businesses beyond TASQ that can be acquired to give it a base for growth in some very attractive *adjacent markets*. Merchant Services can either acquire all of a small organization that it can integrate into its operation, or acquire part of a large enterprise, learn the nature of the business with the acquisition's management still in place, and then selectively ratchet up ownership.

The second approach is the way Merchant Services entered the risk analysis and management business to provide added value for its retail customers. Retailers are susceptible to all manner of fraudulent credit card schemes, for which they bear partial or complete liability. A company called Cardservice International built a business specializing in advising merchants on these issues, and First Data bought a half interest in the business. As soon as Merchant Services was sure that it could leverage its customer relationships and processing acumen in the new field, the company exercised its option to purchase the remaining half of the business.

Another example of this partial acquisition strategy is Merchant Services' entry into ATM networks by purchasing 64 percent of the NYCE network. Automatic teller networks provide the connectivity and processing to handle debit cards at point of sale. Debit cards are growing rapidly in usage in the United States, but still lag far behind their level of use in Europe. They provide a quicker transaction at point of sale and cost less for merchants to process than credit cards.

In NYCE, First Data acquired an established revenue stream, a strong management team, and market know-how that would have taken years to assemble. First Data is now enhancing the growth of the acquisition by bringing all of its own strengths to bear. Adjacent growth remains a large opportunity for the Merchant Services division. Any market that is transactionally intensive but operationally inefficient may be an opportunity for adjacent growth. For example, the credit card transaction model could be applied to airline ticketing and boarding, or to admissions at concerts, movies, and other events. Anywhere there are lots of transactions and people who need to be identified and authorized, the low-cost credit card model might have an advantage.

Why not, for example, convert the healthcare insurance market to a credit card model? Issue a mag stripe card to every enrolled member, place card terminals in every doctor's office, hospital, and pharmacy in the country, and use the card to manage the flow of transactions and information. Authorization would be more difficult, since each health insurer has complex rules about reimbursement, but settlement, charge-back, reconciliation, reporting, and fraud detection would be about the same. It would be a big job, but remember, this is an organization that comfortably manages terminals at three million merchant locations, processes more than ten billion transactions a year, and has 325 million credit cards on file. Taking on a big chunk of the U.S. healthcare system wouldn't be beyond its reach.

So, don't airlines, events, and healthcare seem like ripe adjacencies for growth? And they're only three of many markets that might be convertible to the credit card model.

There's only one catch. There's no large firm out there to acquire. Merchant Services would have to build any adjacency organically and, as we've seen, that's not a current strength of the organization.

Base retention rates in the merchant servicing business are relatively high, principally because the services are provided under multiyear agreements. The fight for contract renewals can be heated, but the incumbent supplier generally has the upper hand. This is because the cost of switching to another supplier is high for both the retailer and the alternative supplier, who must re-equip each location and convert the retailer to a new servicing platform. Merchant Services competes in a low- to moderately churning market that has profited from all these factors, but it still sees opportunity to further improve base retention.

As to *market positioning,* the company covers the whole of the North American market for merchant services. However, CEO Fote and the management team realized that the international market is now the prime growth opportunity, and they need to grow their international presence to match their domestic success. This has become a special focus for growth in the next few years. To lead this effort, Fote has appointed a senior executive, at a peer level to divisional heads, to focus exclusively on international growth for the Card Issuing and Merchant Services divisions.

Card Issuing Services

The biggest challenge for Fote and his management team was to balance the growth portfolio of the Card Issuing Services division. Its recent experience had been typical of a market leader in a declining market.

With its large share in the U.S. card processing market, the division was serving almost every segment. When you are this big, there is only a limited opportunity to pick the faster-growing segments and avoid the decline of the market's core. Favorable *market positioning* just isn't much of an option.

True, the division might try to grow in the small-scale segment of the market, where retailers, nonprofit organizations, and others hand out cards. There was some indication that the small end of the market was not as stormy as the large end, where the big banks, American Express, and other large buyers of processing services could exert maximum leverage on price. But, on balance, the opportunity for Card Issuing Services in the small-issuer segment was also small.

In a declining market, the first instinct is to *retain the base* of existing clients, and Card Issuing Services pays meticulous attention to each account. Not a morning starts without Charlie Fote convening a 6:30 meeting of his top thirty-five executives. In the next sixty minutes, the entire team reviews any major service issues involving key clients across the entire business and discusses remedies, roles, and responsibilities. This focus on the current needs of customers reflects the fact that service problems are the major reason why clients don't renew contracts, even though they devote most of their negotiations to price. The early-morning meetings are one of the many things that has helped First Data to achieve market-leading base retention rates.

Service and value, not contracts, retain customers in a declining market. That's because negotiating power shifts to customers, especially big customers, and they can demand to renegotiate contracts almost at will. If you refuse to reopen, that's the last contract you'll see from that customer.

The team also had to find the business model that would let them win in a commoditizing market. As the market consolidated, contracts were being renewed at lower prices (or perhaps in the disguised form of constant prices with increased service requirements). Unless Card Issuing Services could fund these revenue reductions with productivity gains, they would eat directly into profits. The challenge was to use the division's scale, which is more than 50 percent larger than that of its nearest competitor, to create significant cost advantages through economies of scale. That effort continues.

But not all customers are worth keeping, and the division's managers also had to develop a thorough understanding of the economics of base retention if they were to avoid doing business at unprofitable terms. There is a point in negotiations at which it is better to fold your hand and walk away from a customer than to continue to play, especially in a declining market.

Share gain through in-line acquisitions is usually an important growth discipline in a declining market. But for Card Issuing Services this was a limited option. There were fewer and fewer small competitors to buy, and any large acquisition of a direct competitor was unlikely to pass regulatory review.

That was the bad news. The good news was that most organizations make acquisitions in a declining market so that they can gain economies of scale. Card Issuing Services already had the scale. The division's challenge was simply to extract the economic advantage through cost cuts. If they could achieve the low-cost position in their market, they would be able to grow market share organically. The market was becoming increasingly price-sensitive, and First Data would be able to put the best price on the table.

The division recognized that it had been late to explore *adjacent markets,* where it could leverage its client relationships and its processing know-how. The obvious opportunity was to try other forms of processing for financial institutions, including check processing and loan administration. Another adjacent opportunity would be to provide support for card marketing and consumer management.

A third possibility would be to take over account processing in other industries, such as frequent flyer programs or telecom. The difficulty, of course, is that this opportunity is farther afield and might require Card Issuing Services to make a fundamental change in its processing infrastructure, adjusting to industries it does not yet understand.

First Data's Fourth Leg

Fote and his managers had yet another page in their strategy—one they called "the fourth leg" of growth for First Data. While new lines of business were off-limits for the divisions, no such rule was applied at the corporate level. In addition to strengthening the growth portfolios of the three divisions, the management team created a formal effort to identify attractive markets that might be further afield than an adjacency, but not so far as to be entirely unleveragable with core capabilities. The rule of thumb for adjacencies, as we have seen, is to find a market in which the company's capabilities provide at least 80 percent of the required business model in that market. Just outside that circle lie several markets with robust growth rates, familiar processing requirements, and attractive candidates for acquisition. That last point is an important one. The further afield that First Data ventures into new lines of business, the more important it is that the company enter through an acquisition. That's because it will need deep industry knowledge and experience—and what better way to obtain it than by acquiring a robust participant in the desired market. When all the plans are taken together, they add up to an impressive response to the challenge of growth. The whole company has been energized to expect and demand growth of each other and of the whole enterprise. Each division has been evaluated, its stretch growth objective established, and a plan of attack formed. Charlie Fote's will to succeed, his fierce desire to make First Data the best that it can be, is behind all of this effort, and Charlie himself is out front, leading his troops on to the desired result.

4

The First Discipline: Keep the Growth You Have Already Earned

---

When a customer leaves your company, it is like a tax on growth. Just as taxes cut the bottom line, customer defections come right off the top. Suppose your company is growing by 20 percent per year. If you lose 15 percent of your existing customers each year, that means three quarters of your annual growth does nothing but replace the business you're losing. In effect, you're working until October just to make up the deficit; at the end of the year, your net growth is a measly 5 percent.

The wireless communications industry provides a case in point. Sprint PCS increased its customer base in 2002 by 1.1 million subscribers to 14.9 million, a gain of about 8 percent. The company spent about $2.5 billion on sales, marketing, and equipment subsidies to achieve that growth, or about $2,200 for every customer gained—a lot of money considering that the average monthly bill is only $62. By way of contrast, Nextel enlarged its subscriber base that year by 1.9 million customers—a handsome 22 percent increase—while spending $500 million less than Sprint on sales, marketing, and equipment subsidies.

Why the discrepancy? On the face of it, the answer seems clear: Nextel does a better job of attracting new customers. In fact, the difference between the two companies comes down to base retention.

Sprint PCS managed to lose 42 percent of its customer base in

2002. In order to achieve 8 percent growth, it actually had to sign up 50 percent more customers. Nextel also added 50 percent more customers, but because it lost only 27 percent of its customer base, it ended up with a much higher net growth rate. Had Sprint PCS enjoyed the retention efficiencies of Nextel, it could have saved the extra $750 million it spent attracting replacement customers.

The secondary impacts of poor base retention are evident from this example. Other parts of the growth portfolio need to work double time to make up for the customers that are leaking out of the base retention bucket. That adds to overall costs as well as diminishing overall growth rates. Fully 23 percent of Sprint's revenue was dedicated to gaining market share, yet 84 percent of it—$2.1 billion—was spent simply replacing failures in base retention. And that doesn't include the ancillary costs of starting and stopping so many customer relationships. All told, customer churn probably took $3 billion off Sprint's bottom line.

Forget Loyalty

The conventional wisdom holds that the best way to fix base retention problems is to focus on customer loyalty. In fact, most businesses view loyalty as a kind of Holy Grail. Like knights-errant on an endless quest, managers ride on for years, tilting with competitors, enduring endless rejection, in their pursuit of individuals and organizations that will remain faithful. These people, the theory goes, have a natural tendency to be loyal; once they are in the fold, they can be kept there by giving them superior value.

But the theory is wrong.

The quest for loyal customers is largely wasted effort. And the notion that current customers will remain simply because of bolt-on improvements in a company's value proposition is, as this chapter will demonstrate, naïve. Yes, you must keep customers if you are to consistently achieve double-digit growth. As the first of my five disciplines puts it, you have to retain your customer base. But no, the traditional way of going about that task won't work.

To begin with, let's get something straight: customer loyalty is a contradiction in terms—an oxymoron. If there ever were any customers who would never abandon you for a competitor's product—as we all were told at our father's knee—they are nowhere to be found today. Sentimental loyalty doesn't exist. Companies that have committed to complicated schemes for customer loyalty management don't have much to show for it. Consider Lexus, the luxury car division of Toyota. A few years ago it was being held up as an icon of customer loyalty management. According to Fred Reichheld, the author of *The Loyalty Effect*, "Lexus has built a new business system, engineered from the ground up on the principles of loyalty-based management, and is now on its way to setting record levels of loyalty in the auto industry." At the time, Lexus was enjoying repurchase rates averaging 63 percent for the 1993 and 1994 model years, according to Reichheld, below its target of 75 percent.

Today, according to R. L. Polk, the authority on automobile purchase patterns, only 40 percent of Lexus owners buy another Lexus as their next car. That trails Ford and Chevrolet, both at 56 percent, and Cadillac, at 46 percent. In the thirteen categories of automobiles that Polk tracks, only the Lexus flagship LS430 leads its category, and even there, the repurchase rate is only 25 percent. The repurchase rate for Ford pickups, Cadillac DeVilles, and Buick LeSabres is about 40 percent.

How could things have gone so terribly awry at Lexus?

Another heralded example of loyalty management is Staples, the office supplies retailer. Soon after launching the company in 1986, the management team instituted a program to track individual customers' purchases so that it could calculate customer value and focus its loyalty management efforts on just the right customers. After spending millions of dollars trying to get this business system to work, Staples dropped it in 1995. "Too expensive and complex," said Staples founder Tom Stemberg. The company introduced a smaller, less expensive initiative called Staples Dividends. That, too, was dropped. Now it has an even simpler program called Staples Business Rewards that rebates its largest retail customers up to $15 per month. Clearly, Staples has abandoned its grandiose visions of customer loyalty management.

Or how about the granddaddy of loyalty rewards programs at American Airlines? What has its much-emulated frequent flyer program earned it? Is there any evidence that customers are more loyal to American Airlines than to other carriers? In an industry where price and schedule dominate the purchase decision, what does loyalty really mean? Ed French, president of AAdvantage Marketing Services, has turned his attention to selling frequent flyer miles to other companies as rewards for *their* customers. This is probably a good business plan, since it enables the airline to generate some much-needed revenue, but it no longer has anything to do with loyalty to American Airlines.

The notion of loyalty management has spawned an entire industry. Like American Airlines, more than a dozen companies offer loyalty rewards programs to companies looking for a deal-sweetener for its best customers. These bolt-on programs, though popular, don't have much impact on base retention, since they add only marginally to the overall value proposition of an organization.

But rewards are only one small part of the loyalty management industry. Software to identify, track, and manage customer interactions has become a multibillion-dollar business. Siebel Systems is the leader in this so-called Customer Relationship Management (CRM) software. In addition, scores of consultancies, large and small, offer a range of loyalty services. Customer lifetime value analysis, for example, is a method purported to calculate the impact of customer loyalty on the economics of a company. Customer segmentation is designed to identify inherently loyal customer segments. It's all very appealing stuff, but, unfortunately, most of it has failed to deliver proven results.

Consider Siebel. Founded by Tom Siebel in 1993, the software company peaked in 2001 with revenues of $2 billion. This is how he has described the decision to create CRM: "The problems of sales and customer service had been largely untouched by computer technology. It seemed highly likely that one could use computer technology to establish and maintain customer relationships. It seemed to me there would be an opportunity to build a pretty nice little business here."

His company's Web site extols the benefits of CRM through numerous customer testimonials and case studies. Siebel publishes a research report claiming an 18 percent improvement in base retention among customers using its software. The company also includes an "ROI calculator" on its Web site so that you, too, can calculate what you're missing by not installing Siebel software.

Nucleus Research, a small market research shop in Wellesley, Massachusetts, took the unusual step of contacting all sixty-six of the testimonial companies identified in Siebel's Web site to better understand the benefits of CRM. They got twenty-three of them to talk and, according to Ian Campbell, Nucleus's chief research officer, "An in-depth interview was conducted by phone with a Nucleus research analyst and in most cases with the exact same person Siebel quoted on its Web site." The report says, "The assumption was that because Nucleus was examining customers that Siebel was itself promoting as examples of successful deployments, Nucleus would find customers that had received better-than-average returns." What it found instead was that 61 percent of the customers were convinced that they had yet to achieve a return on investment after two years with the Siebel applications, which cost an average of about $6.6 million over a three-year period. "It is pretty astonishing that these are Siebel reference customers and they are not getting a return on investment," said

Nucleus analyst Rebecca Wettemann. "If you have three best friends and two say you're a jerk, what does that tell you?"

Consultants peddling customer lifetime value (LTV) analysis and loyalty segmentation schemes haven't fared much better. LTV is computed by estimating the stream of profits that a customer will generate over time and discounting that stream for the probability that the customer will be disloyal and leave at some future period and for the time value of money. As math goes, it's a pretty seductive formula. The problem, though, is that it leaves out of the analysis two of the most important ingredients: the viewpoints of the customer and the competitor. As shall be seen in a minute, these are important omissions.

After all, if loyalty is just a label and not an inherent characteristic, then segmenting customers by loyalty doesn't predict very much.

Base Retention Basics

If customer loyalty is a will-o'-the-wisp, what can you rely upon to keep your customers in the fold? Part of the answer, of course, applies to encounters with potential customers as well as existing ones: they all have to be sold on your product. In the following pages, I set forth the three chief principles governing product sales in general, along with the three key matching strategies that companies can—and should—use in dealing with their own customers.

First though, a basic question: how do people decide to buy a product or service? Ideally, they start by assembling the broadest possible set of alternative offers. They then evaluate these choices, using all the pertinent measures of essential value, and carefully weigh each possibility in relation to their own particular requirements, present and future.

That is the way to optimize a buying decision. If a market has a lot of customers who optimize, we describe it as highly efficient. Everyone gets the best available value—or close to it. In the market for airline seats, for instance, online reservation systems make it easy to find the best price or the best schedule available for any trip, so each customer can optimize his or her decision.

While everyone wants to optimize value, the truth is that it can take a lot of effort to search out alternatives, evaluate their offerings, and balance the features that each provides against your needs for value. Retail banking is an example of a market where customers rarely optimize their purchase behavior. Most people have kept the same banking relationship for more than a decade. Yet, survey after survey shows general dissatisfaction with the level of service that retail banks provide, especially in this era of sequential bank mergers. Why do people stay? Do they feel loyal to their retail bank? No. It's simply that most customers see little difference in the value provided by one local bank versus another. They first chose their bank for its location, and as the relationship has lengthened, the difficulty of switching has grown. Why change banks when the small set of alternatives doesn't look any better and the hassle of switching seems pretty great?

Parking lot operators know all about efficient and inefficient customers. The regular customers, who park downtown five days a week, have the time and motivation to do their homework and find the best combination of price and location to fit their needs. That's why parking lots offer very competitive, fairly uniform rates for all-day parking. But those operators also know that the occasional customer, with neither the time nor the motivation to shop for the best deal, will settle for a higher and less efficient deal. That's why the hourly rates vary widely, and at central points they spike outrageously.

Entire brands are sustained by customers who don't purchase very optimally. How else can one explain Tupperware, KB Toys, Pabst beer, and a host of other corporate has-beens? Why do people still buy electronics from Circuit City, or Sears for that matter, when they know there are better deals and better information available on the Internet? Because that is their habit, and the familiar is the path of least resistance. Why do corporations continue to procure local services without full competitive bidding? Their attention is focused on the big-ticket or high-volume purchases, so the little stuff is bought satisfactorily, but not optimally.

To win new customers and hold onto the old ones, companies must heed the first principle of base retention: shape the customers' value criteria. Successful companies are often as effective at influencing the purchase decision as they are at delivering superior customer value. They often try to keep their customers focused on the dimensions of value in which they excel.

As one of the largest radio advertisers in the country, David Oreck has relentlessly pounded home one aspect of his product with advertising touting "the Oreck eight-pound vacuum." Does this feature matter? *Consumer Reports* ranks weight as one of only seven criteria that it considers (including price, noise, and cleaning efficiency) and ranks Oreck vacuums in the middle of the pack. Oreck's clever promotion has influenced customers and potential customers to place the weight of a vacuum high on their priority list. By stressing the one feature at which his product stands out and influencing customers to more highly value this feature, Oreck has achieved years of double-digit growth.

In responding to the needs of existing customers, in shaping their value criteria, incumbent companies have a major weapon at their disposal. They have more information about their customers than any competitor could have.

Insiders are always in the know. That's one power of incumbency. What value criteria matter most to a customer, how decisions get made, who's important to the purchase decision and who's not—all of this intelligence allows an incumbent to trade on inside information. With it the incumbent is able to craft a more effective account strategy that responds to a customer's needs and services the relationship in a far more efficient manner. No wasted motion, no missteps, fewer uncertainties.

A master at using its incumbency to gather information and build effective account plans is Oracle. The software giant may initially win the customer with its database offering, but it attacks applications and integration services opportunities as soon as its sales team has gathered up enough information about the customer to know what applications are being considered for replacement, what's wrong with the current system, and, most importantly, whose agendas are being furthered by the contemplated purchase.

By following the first principle of base retention—shape customers' value criteria—and by applying its information advantage, Oracle has built an enviable record of base retention. The second principle of base retention is to increase switching costs. It speaks to that moment of decision when companies and individuals find themselves tempted to leave the fold and take their business to another vendor or retailer. Your competitor wants to steal them away with attractive value that beats your offer, but you have an ace up your sleeve. For that customer to enjoy the value proposition of a new supplier, it must incur the cost, aggravation, and inconvenience of switching. If you've done a diligent job entangling that customer, those switching costs can be a formidable barrier.

Here again, incumbency has its advantages, this time in economic clout. By exercising it with skill and imagination, incumbents can achieve the upper hand both with their customers and with competitors, particularly in those markets where switching costs are significant. That's because the customer must deduct the cost of switching from any alternative value proposition offered. An incumbent doesn't have to match a competitor's deal; its value proposition simply has to be less than the cost of switching to the competitor's deal. The competitor has to offer not just better value, but enough better value to overcome the cost of switching.

Why, for example, do telecommunications providers, credit card companies, and software producers routinely offer their best deals to attract new customers rather than reward their current ones? On the face of it, that will alienate current customers and lead them to defect. Don't existing customers deserve a better deal than newcomers?

Viewed through the harsh lens of incumbent economics, the answer is no. This is not a comfortable conclusion, but it is one that explains why many companies offer better deals to attract new clients than they offer to their best, retained customers. For years, AT&T, WorldCom, and other long-distance telecommunications providers have neglected to tell current customers about lower-cost plans being marketed to potential customers. The companies want to keep existing customers who buy high-feature, high-margin service from down-shifting to a lower-margin service. If such a customer threatens to leave, the better deal will be offered—but not until then.

The third of my principles of base retention is to narrow customers' alternatives. It addresses a universal problem confronting buyers and sellers alike: there are so many products to choose from. If you are trolling for new customers, the challenge becomes, how can you differentiate your product from all the others? If you are trying to hold on to existing customers, you face the same concern since new competitive products are constantly making their appearance.

The solution: cut back on the number of products against which customers measure your offering.

In the old days, planning a plane trip was a hassle with all those different airlines and their different times of departure and ticket-cost variations. A traveler had too many alternatives. A most inefficient market.

Then along came American Airlines, which developed the first truly efficient reservation system, which was eventually widely copied. The result was to shift power to consumers, arming them with almost perfect information on prices and schedules to optimize their purchase decisions. Suddenly, the market was efficient and the consumers could narrow their choices to the one or two airlines that best met their needs. Good news for travelers, but bad for the industry, which was whipsawed by these übershoppers into chronically underpricing and overscheduling its product.

For a prime example of a company positively influencing the decision process by narrowing the alternatives, consider the Bose Corporation. Founded by Dr. Amar Bose, a Massachusetts Institute of Technology professor, in 1964, the Massachusetts-based audio-equipment manufacturer had revenues of more than $1.2 billion in 2002.

Bose is a legendary marketer, having battled Sony, Yamaha, Matsushita, and other Japanese enterprises in the core of their strength, consumer electronics. His success owes as much to his ability to manage his customers' purchase process as to its fine offerings. Rule number one for Bose has been to narrow the range of products against which his are compared. He avoids Best Buy, Circuit City, and most other mass and Internet retailers where his goods would be up against a large assortment of other brands. Instead, the company's products show up at specialty retailers such as Neiman Marcus and Sharper Image, which give Bose exclusive placement. The company also sells directly to consumers, through its own stores, direct-mail response, print advertising, and ubiquitous demonstration sites in airports and other sites nationwide. Bose has built a formidable set of channels that studiously avoid comparisons. The demonstration sites are a particularly clever and effective channel, since any audio product is bound to sound pretty good when the background noise of an airport or shopping mall is the only available comparison.

Incumbents have a special advantage, and powerful strategic opportunity, in their effort to follow the narrowed alternatives principle. They can use their unique influence on their customers to dictate their product choices.

Incumbents' access to their customers and the credibility and trust they have established ensure them of an influence far beyond that granted to most outsiders. This privileged position can be used to cement an account relationship for years to come.

Perhaps the master of incumbent influence is McKinsey, the venerable consulting shop. Though it has had significant adverse publicity for its role in the meltdowns at Enron, Kmart, Swissair, and Global Crossing, its relationship with core customers such as Siemens, Johnson & Johnson, and General Motors appears unshaken.

The organization's involvement in these matters has thrown open a window on McKinsey's influence. *Business Week* quoted one former Enron senior executive, for example, as saying that McKinsey consultants had clout all through the organization. "They were all over the place," he said. "They were sitting with us every step of the way."

That kind of influence can be used to shape the customer's value criteria, to raise the cost of switching to another consultant, or (as Klaus Kleinfeld, CEO of Siemens, admits) to reduce the alternatives that are even given consideration. "You have lunch. You have dinner. And then projects evolve. Very often, competitive bidding doesn't happen."

Base Retention Strategies

In the pages that follow, I have set forth four diverse base retention tactics that are illustrated through the case histories of a variety of companies. In every case, though, the tactics fulfill the three principles just discussed, and their attendant strategies: they shape the customers' value criteria, increase their switching costs, and narrow their alternatives. Each strategy makes the most of the powerful advantages of incumbency to gain insider information about the customer, exercise economic advantage over competitors, and have undue influence over customer opinions.

Before I start, though, a word of caution: all the base retention strategies in the world cannot keep your customers in the fold unless you simultaneously improve your value proposition. All of us have become used to rapidly rising value in the goods we buy; for example, the cars of ten or twenty years ago were far less reliable, durable, safe, or efficient than the automobiles we get today—and, adjusted for inflation, today's models don't even cost much more. The same thing has happened in technology, housing, and clothing, and someday may even happen in professional services.

So, to keep your customers, particularly your übershoppers— those hardliners who get the most out of every dollar by poring over *Consumer Reports,* searching the Internet, haggling over prices, and registering their warranties—you have to meet their ever-rising expectations. In fact, you have to exceed those expectations. If a customer gets exactly the benefits she pays for, no value has been delivered. Value is perceived only when she gets more than she expected for her money.

Now, let's examine those base retention tactics.

Make Your Services Sticky

If you can entice customers into complex relationships, they will be reluctant to go through the hassle of undoing those relationships in order to leave—and you will have taken a giant step toward base retention.

Your motivation should be clear: you want to entangle customers to create enough immediate economic value for them that no competitor will be able to come up with a big enough offer to outweigh their switching costs. Happily, customers are far more conscious of the benefits of each new strand of the tangle than they are of its potential penalties in some distant future. Switching costs tend to be perceived as a deferred expense that can be deferred indefinitely.

When Jeffrey Immelt took over as CEO of General Electric, one of the first programs he pushed was a companywide initiative entitled "At the Customer, for the Customer" or ACFC. It was intended to make every GE division a kind of consultant for its customers, providing free help and advice to improve their operations—and, not incidentally, to entangle them with their benevolent supplier.

Free consulting is just the tip of the iceberg, though. GE, in most of its divisions, has built substantial fee-for-service businesses that act as paid consultants to its clients. In this role it has the opportunity to help set the management agenda for change, offer high-quality in-house educational programs, and take part in implementing process and technology improvements for the customer. Services have been wrapped around most of GE's products to improve the total impact that GE can have on customer results and to simultaneously give GE a privileged position that grows out of an ever-more-entangled customer relationship.

Consider the case of GE Medical Systems, which just happens to be the business Jeff Immelt was running before he ascended to the top job. This $9 billion operation sells complex medical instruments for diagnostic imaging, cardiology, surgical support, and patient monitoring. The ultrasound business alone brings in $1 billion a year. But also buried within GE Medical is a lucrative services business growing at better than 30 percent a year. GE Medical manages the entire life cycle of its equipment for clients—capital planning, financing, performance monitoring, maintenance, upgrades, even disposal. Beyond those typical product services, GE Medical has established a large management-consulting capability that can help its hospital clients improve their revenue generation, identify and enact operational improvements using GE's Six Sigma methodology, fine-tune clinical performance, and improve the quality of clinical outcomes. It also offers extensive educational services, from technical training in diagnostic imaging to leadership development for teams of hospital administrators.

More recently, it has embarked on an ambitious growth strategy in hospital information technology. In August 2000, GE formed the

Medical Systems Information Technology unit to expand its reach into managing the flow of clinical information within hospitals. Already the division is generating annual sales of $1.5 billion. GE aims to marry the clinical areas of a hospital with the front and back ends: registration and billing. The price of success, of course, is that no hospital will ever be able to afford to switch to Siemens, GE's chief competitor, once GE has burrowed into its core medical and business processes.

GE Medical's services strategy has been emulated in three other divisions that sell complex products: power systems, aircraft engines, and transportation, which includes the company's locomotive business. For example, in the aircraft engines group, GE lends teams of Six Sigma experts to airlines for use in improving processes in any area, from the tire shop to flight scheduling. This free consulting has netted the airlines some $400 million in cost savings so far, according to Roger Seager, the group's vice president of marketing and sales. The program was initiated after customers began commenting, "You're always telling us how great Six Sigma is. Why don't you show us what it means?" Seager says that GE has now done thousands of these programs. He believes the company is ahead of any other in allocating so many resources to customer support. Services now generate more than $20 billion annually for GE.

The evolution of GE Medical's services strategy has had a profound impact on the division's ability to retain its base of customers in the products business. For starters, all that service creates the kind of entanglement that raises switching costs, making it very expensive for any customer to leave and creating a significant impediment for competitors. It is a classic example of a company pursuing the second principle of base retention, increasing the switching cost, by providing valuable, but entangling, services. Its policy has insulated GE from low-price competition or a temporary lag in its product leadership. Here's what Jeff Immelt has to say: "These are long-term, intimate customer commitments, where our rewards are tied to customer success. . . . [It] gets GE on the same side as the customers by linking their future success to our own."

The entanglement policy also supports the other two base retention principles. All these services, from maintaining equipment on the clinical floor to delivering a customer leadership seminar, yield important information about the account, enabling GE to shape customers' value criteria. In addition, by using its growing influence on the entangled customer, the company effectively reduces the alternatives the customer can consider in making a purchase decision. GE has created a virtuous cycle of entanglement.

It is a natural for suppliers of complex commercial or financial products to develop a service strategy that supports base retention, because complex products create many opportunities to assist the client. Few companies, though, have been able to build the depth of services that GE has created because few companies are ahead of their clients in such a broad range of capabilities.

On the consumer front, General Motors has pioneered On*Star telematics technology that could provide the infrastructure for similar services in the future. Through telematics, automobile manufacturers can provide a host of in-car services, entangling customers with such features as roadside assistance, driving directions, and even restaurant reservations, once they have accumulated intimate knowledge of customers' habits and tastes. Also, for the first time, auto manufacturers have the ability to bypass dealers and develop a direct relationship with their customers.

At the same time, the system allows them to collect detailed information on automobile performance and customers' driving habits. That information is potentially a treasure trove for shaping the value criteria of automobile customers. It remains to be seen whether General Motors will be able to develop the type of sticky, value-added services that will improve base retention, enhancing its cars' repurchase rate. With Daimler Benz, Ford, and others rolling out similar technologies, GM doesn't have much time.

Tailor Your Offering

Information is cheap these days. Many companies have collected masses of data about their customers. Right now, somewhere in the bowels of a data center, the grocery store in your neighborhood has probably stored your family's entire purchase history. The problem is, the store can't figure out what to do with it. Remember Staples' early efforts at loyalty cards? Staples replaced them with a much simpler program when it realized the difficulty of turning its ambitions into reality. Owning information and not knowing how to use it is an all-too-familiar business experience.

Casino operator Harrah's Entertainment, based in Las Vegas, also had big dreams about taking advantage of incumbency to gather information about customers and using it to shape the customers' value criteria. But, in Harrah's case, the dreams were realized. The key to its base retention strategy has been to understand customer behaviors, motivations, and value judgments so well that it can personalize the entertainment experience for its best customers. Thus, the company can create an offering that a customer is hard-pressed to find elsewhere.

Harrah's was founded in Reno, Nevada, by the legendary operator Bill Harrah in 1937 and now operates twenty-six casinos in twelve states. At more than $4 billion in revenues, Harrah's has grown revenues, gross profits, and net profits at an average rate of more than 20 percent since 1997. An MIT-trained Ph.D. economist named Gary Loveman runs the company. Loveman has used his skills to install sophisticated systems for gathering and analyzing data about his best customers and then used that information to customize the entertainment experience that his organization can provide to each of them.

"My approach was based on a very simple realization," said Gary Loveman. "We learned that of all the casino customers who visited Harrah's once a year or more, we got 36 cents of their gaming dollar. So the fundamental issue was not getting more people to gamble, or even getting more people to know our name, but increasing the percentage of time our customers spend at a Harrah's casino. . . . We rallied everything around the notion that we had to get that percentage up."

The result? In four years he has raised the percentage that Harrah's collects from its customers' gaming dollars from 36 percent to 42 percent. The company's customers are more often choosing to come back to Harrah's for their next gaming experience. Among Harrah's best customers—let's call them the big losers—retention is even stronger.

The key to Loveman's system is the Total Rewards card that gives customers prizes every time they pull a slot machine lever, see a show, or have a meal. That allows the company to collect invaluable information about customers' behavior, and Loveman's training as an economist has allowed him to expand his company's ability to turn that data into actionable insight. With the help of clever tools that estimate the gaming potential of each customer—what he or she might be spending elsewhere—Harrah's is able to arm itself with the information that it needs to influence the customer's repurchase decision.

Perhaps the most difficult part of Loveman's strategy has been execution. "When I got to Harrah's it struck me over and over again how relatively easy the big thinking is, and how daunting the execution is," Loveman recalled. "It's an amazingly complex service-delivery process. You're lodging people, you're feeding people, parking their cars, entertaining them, making travel plans for them—all these things are mixed together with the gaming."

Harrah's is in the business of providing the best entertainment experience for its customers, and every customer is different. Sure, they all want to win at the gaming tables, but there's a wide range of other entertainment options as well. Harrah's has used the incumbent's access to customer information to create customized entertainment experiences and in a small way that has raised the switching costs of its customers. They probably don't think of it that way; instead they just feel that the casino down the street feels a little less like "home" and requires that customers be a little more assertive to get the entertainment and services they want. The careful tracking of each customer's spending potential also provides a profile of the customer's gambling habits throughout the year. That way, Harrah's can get customers to think about the long term, arranging for their next visit even before they leave the casino. Simple, but effective base retention.

As the numbers attest, Loveman's strategy for creating a custom entertainment experience for his best customers has paid off handsomely in base retention. More of his best customers' money is being spent at his casinos rather than at the competitors just down the street.

Preempt Defections

What if you could tell when a customer was about to leave you? What if you could know why it was happening and how to create just the right response to prevent it from happening?

Lots of companies have the potential to achieve that goal. In one part of the organization they know that the customer is disgruntled—with service that has gone awry, with a price he or she doesn't think is competitive, with a product that hasn't performed as expected—but that information is never communicated to another part of the company that can do something about it. Or if the information is transferred, it never gets acted on.

It's hard to believe how ineffective companies are at proactively managing customer defections. Perhaps it is because three things have to go right for a company to be able to anticipate and preempt a customer defection. First, it has to be able to predict the event with some accuracy. Second, it has to be able to fashion an effective response that overcomes the cause of the imminent defection. Finally, the company has to be able to effectively execute the response.

That might explain why proactive management of customer defections is so rare, even in situations where an imminent defection is quite obvious. For example, an automobile lease is nearing its end. What kind of interaction does the typical manufacturer have with the customer at this point? A discussion of a new lease, perhaps, or the purchase of a new car? No. They prefer to focus on the possible excessive wear and tear on the vehicle that might require adjustments to the final cost of the current lease. The automobile companies have the information but are unable to fashion and execute the right response.

One industry is a particular standout at disregarding signals that the customer is leaving—the mortgage industry. Try this. Call up your mortgage company and ask it to compute the payoff for your mortgage. That's a pretty clear signal that you're considering leaving. Now wait for the sales call inquiring about your need for a new mortgage. Unless your mortgage is with Washington Mutual, the great likelihood is that you won't be getting that call.

Washington Mutual, known to its employees as WaMu, is a $15 billion financial-services organization focused on consumers and small businesses. Its two major business units are banking and mortgages. Through organic means and a series of acquisitions it has grown to be the largest originator and servicer of mortgage loans in the country—four million of them at last count with a value of more than three quarters of a trillion dollars. That's a lot of mortgages. Led by Kerry Killinger for more than a dozen years, the company has generated consistent double-digit growth in revenues, gross profits, and earnings.

Killinger's mortgage team has installed the industry's most advanced system of people, processes, and technology for identifying customers who are likely to refinance their mortgages. This allows WaMu to contact those customers before they have gone somewhere else. The system also helps to identify why they may be motivated to refinance, and that information is used to help select the appropriate response. Thus, WaMu can usually bring to customers a new mortgage plan before they have begun to actively search out their refinancing options.

The basic information that WaMu uses to predict customer refinancing is the same information available to every mortgage company. After all, people usually refinance for one of three reasons: to get a better interest rate, to take out some of the equity that they've built up in their home, or to buy a different house. By tracking interest rates, house values, payment patterns, service inquiries, and the life-stage needs of individual households, a lot of refinancing can be predicted.

The real power in WaMu's approach is its ability to fashion an effective response to this information. The motto of the mortgage group is "The Power of Yes," which on the face of it appears to be just another bit of banking hyperbole. After all, lenders can't say yes to everyone. Lots of people don't qualify for mortgages.

But WaMu understands how the time frame of customers can affect their switching costs in evaluating a mortgage. Is this a starter home that will likely be kept for only three to five years? Or is it the dream house that will be held for several decades? That's important, because there is little point in paying more to lock in a mortgage that is likely to be refinanced in only a few years.

WaMu has developed a very wide range of mortgage products that broadens its ability to say yes. For example, it has one interest-only mortgage product aimed at customers who are thirty-five to forty-five years old and have accumulated significant equity in their current house and want to jump up to the next level of home. WaMu knows that these folks are a good risk, but need a little help making the payments in the first few years. Other products, aimed at equally narrow customer needs, are intended to blanket the entire range of market needs. The company is continually investing in new products to adjust to the ever-changing needs of the marketplace.

WaMu's efforts at base retention really generalize into three buckets. First, the organization uses its incumbency to gather information about its customers that is not available to competitors. It knows their payment histories, it knows about their service inquiries, and it knows how far their current mortgage is from best available value. Second, the company has built a set of products targeted at ever-narrower customer situations. Third, it has put together the people, processes, and technology to execute its strategy in real time, ahead of the customer's decision cycle.

Some companies have also used similar systems to anticipate and avoid customer defections because of major service gaffes. The cold slap of bad value can lead even the laziest customers to consider alternate suppliers that wouldn't normally be in their search set. That's why it pays to follow the key principles and strategies of base retention, using your inside information to detect potential defectors and shaping their value criteria to keep them in the fold.

Bond with Customers

Whenever and wherever individuals and organizations make decisions, emotion is a part of the equation. The emotional element may be large or small, positive or negative, but you can be sure it's there. Your customers' decisions to stay or buy elsewhere are influenced by their relationship with your company.

That scenario plays out on the front line. The interpersonal and emotional bonds between an account manager and a buyer, a consumer and a salesperson, can be used to overcome a weakness in value or an insurgent competitor's offer. But the most frequent intrusion of emotion for most of us is in our interactions with brands.

As we have seen, most customers, under most circumstances, won't evaluate a full range of alternative products when making a re-purchase decision. The smaller the purchase, the less there is at stake, so the narrower the evaluation. That's one of the reasons why brands are so important for everyday consumer items. A company's brand is a shorthand statement of its value commitment to the customer. Whether it is McDonald's, Kellogg's, Sony, or Wal-Mart, we all un-derstand what type and level of value we can expect from that brand. Unknowingly—and I do mean unknowingly—customers cut branded sellers some slack. They don't have to prove that the value is there; it is assumed.

And brand operates not just at the rational level to communicate value. It can also *create* value by packing significant emotional wallop. Why do people drink Starbucks? Is it because of the taste of the cof-fee or the statement that a Starbucks cup makes about the customer? Do people ride Harleys because they're a better motorbike or because a Harley expresses who they are? Do electricians prefer Greenlee tools because they are better than the imports or because "real electricians use Greenlee"? Do people send Hallmark cards because the card is a great value or because it is a safe brand with which to communicate emotion?

These and other great consumer marketing companies continue to demonstrate the power of brands. Starbucks Coffee, Harley Davidson motorcycles, Greenlee electrical tools, and Hallmark greeting cards all use brand to create an emotional bond with their customers that has value distinct from the practical value of the product. One believes in this value that brands can create to the same extent that one believes that psychiatrists are real doctors.

Powerful brands also declare their uniqueness in a sea of medioc-rity. What better way to discourage customers from making compar-isons than to simply declare, as Hallmark has done, "When you care enough to send the very best," or, as Harley states, "The road starts here." Using their built-in influence over their customers, these brand leaders have narrowed their customers' alternatives. And each of them has delivered double-digit growth over a long period of time.

Consider Apple Computer, another example of effective brand emotion used to retain base customers. Apple's not a growth story; it's more a story about survival against all odds—the little computer company that stood up to the combined might of Microsoft, Intel, Dell, and the rest of the PC industry and tenaciously held on to most of its customer base. That's why it's an interesting example of the power of incumbency in base retention. Apple has used its incumbency to deeply understand its customers' practical and emotional value needs. Then, through a series of award-wining advertising campaigns, Apple has talked to its customers about why they made the right decision to buy a Mac and enlisted them as active participants in the fight against the PC. How could customers not repurchase a Mac when they've already taken sides in the struggle?

Unlike almost any of its competitors, Apple has gotten to know its customers very, very well—the kinds of jobs they hold as educators and creative professionals, what motivates them to buy an iMac, and what makes them tick as people. Like Starbucks drinkers, Apple customers are making a loud statement about themselves—they are creative, independent thinkers, not afraid to break from the herd.

Apple's ad campaigns reinforce the validity of its customers' decisions. The "Think Different" campaign honored many of the creative geniuses who changed the world in the past century, including Albert Einstein, Mohandas Gandhi, Pablo Picasso, and Martin Luther King. " 'Think Different' celebrates the soul of the Apple brand—that creative people with passion can change the world for the better," said Steve Jobs, Apple's founder and CEO. How could anyone have buyer's regret standing in the company of Einstein, Gandhi, Picasso, and King?

The language of the ads ingeniously supports that theme: "Here's to the crazy ones. The misfits. The rebels. The troublemakers. The round pegs in the square holes. The ones who see things differently. They're not fond of rules. And they have no respect for the status quo. You can praise them, disagree with them, quote them, disbelieve them, glorify or vilify them. About the only thing you can't do is ignore them. Because they change things. They invent. They imagine. They heal. They explore. They create. They inspire. They push the human race forward. . . . We make tools for these kinds of people. While some see them as the crazy ones, we see genius. Because the people who are crazy enough to think they can change the world, are the ones who do."

Apple reinforces its customers' commitment to the company by enlisting them as emotional combatants in Apple's fight. The "Real People" campaign Apple launched in 2002 featured real customers who have switched from PCs to the Macintosh. The story they tell is all about the importance of ease of use, something Apple happens to excel at.

That combination of shaping customers' value criteria while simultaneously appealing to their emotions has proven successful for any number of companies seeking to retain their customer base.

Yet there is a danger in relying too heavily on emotion. Recent academic research has found that sellers systematically overestimate the power of their relationships with customers and that customers consider price and switching costs to be much more significant factors in whether to stay or switch suppliers. Studies of brand power have reached the same conclusion. Brand emotion still matters, but less today because of the ready availability to customers of information with which to make rational comparisons of products. Brands on the rise today, such as Dell, Nokia, and Google, tend to be buttressed by solid, rational value leadership rather than emotional appeal.

The growing level of customers' interest in superior value is a phenomenon of our time, and so is their growing skill at finding it. Not since the days when buyers could see and examine the entire universe of their possible purchases in the town square has it been so easy for people to shop carefully and intelligently. Sellers deluge buyers with mailings and television ads and spread out their offerings and prices on the Internet. Web sites are specifically designed to enable customers to compare and contrast a huge range of potential purchases.

Luckily for business, though, most customers and companies are not übershoppers. Their decisions are shaped by all sorts of influences other than the quality and price of a product or service. They are still inefficient shoppers, and they are still susceptible to the base retention principles and strategies set forth in this chapter. Were it otherwise, consistent double-digit growth would be even more difficult to come by.

In the chapter ahead, I discuss the second of the five growth disciplines, gaining market share at the expense of your rivals. That requires a decidedly different approach than base retention. You have to give their customers convincing reasons to jump ship, which may mean a major change in product quality or price—anything that will lower their switching cost. And then you have to find ways to let them know about it.

5

The Second Discipline:
Take Business from Your Competitors

Just before Christmas of 2002, Stelios Haji-Ioannou listened intently as the head of Boeing Commercial Aircraft made his best and final offer. Boeing was trying to win a coveted order for 120 airplanes from easyJet, the discount airline that Haji-Ioannou had founded seven years earlier. After taking over its British rival, Go, easyJet was the biggest kid on the European discount-airline block, and this one order was going to make or break the year for Boeing or its archrival, Airbus.

"This is the deal of the century—take it now or it will never be repeated," the Boeing executive said, Haji-Ioannou recalls. Boeing desperately needed this order. It had booked fewer orders than Airbus in two of the past three years and was in danger of falling behind on deliveries as well. Boeing had started off the year well, garnering a one-hundred-jet order from Ryanair, easyJet's main competitor, in the first quarter. And Boeing was the incumbent at easyJet, which already flew sixty-four of its 737s and had another fourteen on order. In fact, Boeing owned 100 percent of the discount-airline business in Europe, where startups had taken a page right out of Southwest Airline's playbook by standardizing on the Boeing 737.

One week later, Boeing got the answer it wasn't looking for: easyJet gave Airbus the order.

How did Airbus manage this triumph over America's perennial leader in exports? The company did it the old-fashioned way, by delivering better value. As easyJet's Haji-Ioannou put it, "At the end of the day 'low-cost' companies remain low-cost by not wasting money."

By choosing Airbus, easyJet believes that it will achieve a 10 percent saving on the cost of running its aircraft. Part of that saving will come from a hefty discount that Airbus put on the table to win the order. In addition, Airbus agreed to pick up the incremental costs of operating two airplane models in the easyJet fleet, including extra pilot training and maintenance. Thus, the switching costs that Boeing, as the incumbent, could usually count on to keep its customer in the fold were swept off the table.

The final tally for 2002: Airbus booked twenty-three more orders than Boeing's 221. And in 2004, for the first time, Airbus will deliver more commercial jets to customers than anyone else in the world. That's quite a swing, considering that Boeing delivered 60 percent more jets than Airbus as recently as 2001.

As those figures make clear, Airbus's triumph in winning the easyJet order cannot be dismissed as just another example of a company buying market share with an unsustainable offer. Any business can be the value leader for a day, a week, or even a month. But this win is just the latest in a string of market share victories that has enabled Airbus to emerge from nowhere to take the lead in the commercial-airplane industry.

Founded in 1975 as a European consortium of French, German, Spanish, and British companies, Airbus has succeeded at the expense of Boeing, and of Lockheed and McDonald Douglas, both of which have abandoned the market. Now an independent company, Airbus has steadily increased its share of new airplane orders to 31 percent of the market in 1996 and 54 percent in 2002. Only once since 1999, in 2000, when Boeing scooped up 117 orders for its new 777, did Boeing come out on top in this contest. Those orders are now translating into deliveries in this long-cycle industry; Airbus may have the delivery lead for many years to come.

The Toughest Way to Grow

So, if you want to grow your business at double-digit rates, why not, like Airbus, rely on market share gain? Because stealing customers from your competitors can be the toughest, nastiest revenue you'll ever book. No company gives up market share without a struggle. Often it's a bare-knuckle, eye-to-eye slugfest; everyone is bloodied, and there's only one winner.

There are industries where the sport is relatively gentlemanly—consumer packaged goods, for instance. Market share wars in that industry usually amount to a lot of pushing and shoving at the line of scrimmage, with not a lot of field gain to show for it. In a good year, Pepsi might take a point of market share from Coke. Procter & Gamble might double that gain over Unilever. But, that's about it. Both parties know that if they really take the gloves off, neither of them will win. Price wars are so, well, unseemly, it seems.

The market share stalemates that you see in consumer packaged goods are typical of industries where everyone has just about the same operating model. Once you cut through the difference in hype and culture, any Coca-Cola manager would be perfectly at home in the same role at Pepsi. A Unilever executive would be right at home at P&G because both companies have designed their businesses to operate the same way. Hence, they produce the same result. Without an advantaged operating model, the only way to win market share with superior customer value is to take it out of profits, and that's neither sustainable nor rational. It is, of course, precisely what happened in recent years in the telecommunications industry. WorldCom, Qwest, and a host of others were cooking the books to hide the losses that were buying market share gains. Eventually, they had to pay the piper.

As tough as it is to gain market share, it's easy to lose it. Companies do it all the time by falling behind the pack and getting pounded into the ground. Look at Ford Motor Company. In the past five years it has lost about 10 percent of the huge U.S. market for cars and light trucks. It took a lot of mistakes for market share to erode this quickly. First, Ford mishandled the Firestone tire crisis, making it plainly evident that the customer wasn't job number one at Ford. Next, the company mismanaged new-product development so that its most popular models today look like aging relics of a glorious past. The Taurus and Explorer, once category leaders, are having trouble staying even. Finally, Ford has hit the wall financially, losing $6.5 billion over the course of 2001 and 2002 and reducing its credit rating to just one tick above junk status.

Motorola has suffered a similar fate. Its share of the mobile-telephone market has slid from more than 50 percent to about 16 percent, while Nokia, Samsung, and Siemens have all gained. It is a sad story about a company squandering its dominance in wireless technology.

But, generally speaking, companies don't lose market share so much as they are forced to yield it to a superior force. Their customers depart because competitors have stolen them away. This chapter tells you how to make that happen.

Market share growth is all about how to give the other guy a base retention problem. It is the base retention discipline in reverse, but with one important difference. Some wily companies, employing the advantages of incumbency and enjoying a customer base of inefficient shoppers, are able to hold onto market share without demonstrating value leadership. What they cannot do, except in rare circumstances, is increase their share.

Take Market Share

You have decided, despite the perils noted above, to follow the second growth discipline, devoting your company's resources, human and financial, to raiding your competitors' customer base. There are two basic ways you can go. You can seek to overcome the advantages that incumbency gives your rivals and directly challenge them on the basis of superior product or service value. Or you can go whole hog and simply buy market share by buying your competitors. Let's first examine how to build market share.

Blunt Their Advantages

In the last chapter we saw that incumbents enjoy three special benefits: they have greater access to information about their customers; they have greater economic clout with their customers; they can exert greater influence on their customers.

These advantages can be overcome. A competitor can develop better customer information. Or apply greater economic pressure. Or exert more influence. But as an outsider, all these things will require superior effort and insight. Capital One and Procter & Gamble illustrate how to blunt the incumbents' advantages.

Consider customer information. The average retail bank is clearly in an advantaged position when it comes to understanding its customers' needs for financial services. After all, it knows what services its customers are using; it can peer into their accounts, assess the pattern of usage, and collect personal financial information.

But Capital One, the direct marketer of credit cards based in Falls Church, Virginia, has figured out how to know more than its rivals about their customers' credit card needs. And that helped Capital One to capture more than ten million additional customer accounts in 2001 and almost forty million new accounts since it was spun out of Signet bank in 1994. Most of those accounts came right out of the customer base of local banks.

Starting from nowhere, Capital One has catapulted itself to the number-six spot in the highly fragmented credit card market with about a 6 percent share. Its central strategy for market share gain has been what it calls its Information Based Strategy (IBS). The company has assembled a massive base of customer data on nearly every household in the United States. The information allows Capital One to understand household patterns of credit card use and responsiveness to various card features. For example, the company knows which households are highly interest-rate sensitive and will switch for a better deal. It knows which households use and value the extra features that come with gold or platinum status and which households do not. It knows about the range of cards that a household head carries in his or her wallet and why certain ones get used over others. The company is also able to use its information base to scientifically test new card variations before taking them to market, and its computer systems allow it to tailor the product features to the individual customer. The result: Capital One knows the motivations and behaviors of credit card customers better than the banks that already "own" those customers.

Other businesses have leveled the playing field with incumbents by using their economic clout to remove switching-cost barriers. As we saw, Airbus chose to underwrite the cost of easyJet's move away from Boeing, using its financial resources to offer a major discount and reimburse its customer for its extra maintenance and training expenditures. That may be a very expensive subsidy in the long run.

Fidelity and Schwab, as well as Ameritrade, have made hay in the race to gain 401(k) investment accounts from more traditional investment advisors by using their muscle to make a switch hassle-free. Open a new account, give them your old 401(k) account information, and they'll take care of the rest.

Procter & Gamble provides an interesting example of how a competitor can overcome the influence advantage of an incumbent. P&G has formed a new marketing unit, called Tremor, to gather together more than two hundred thousand teenagers who are its competitors' best customers. These kids have been chosen after extensive research by P&G to determine the traits of opinion-setting teens. The teens are being given samples of Cover Girl and Old Spice products that are in development; they then provide feedback to help the company better understand teen needs. P&G hopes to establish regular e-mail communications with these teens as a way to maintain its influence over their buying opinions. The real power of this program, P&G hopes, is that its huge panel of teens will spread a positive vibe about P&G products. How could an incumbent competitor ever compete with the opinions of two hundred thousand teenagers who believe that P&G *really* listens to them?

It is possible, as the examples above demonstrate, but outwitting and outperforming competitors in the very areas where they have built-in advantages is tough duty. It demands a level of creativity and commitment that most companies cannot achieve—or maintain. And because the task is so difficult, the gains, if and when they come, are likely to be incremental. That makes for a lopsided cost/benefit ratio.

It goes without saying that you are going to have to match the customer value offered by the competitor you target. Customers are not apt to jump ship, no matter how much you blunt the incumbent's advantages, if your product or service is inferior to what they've been getting or if your prices are out of sight.

And that leads us to the second strategy, namely, if you want to chalk up really sizable, sustainable share gain, the odds are you will do far better by offering rivals' customers truly superior value.

Deliver Far Better Value

In general, incumbent companies prefer to keep their markets inefficient as a defense against invasion. They try to stave off price transparency and product comparability. That is why car dealers have turned price into a game and built their profits into financing and add-ons. It is why many large industrial products companies were unwilling to participate in open electronic markets. It's why, when you use Travelocity, a spin-off of American Airlines, to check on flights from Providence to Baltimore, you won't find any of Southwest Airline's dozen daily flights listed.

These tricks of incumbency are intended to keep customers uninformed—and in some markets it works, at least for a while. But eventually, if not sooner, customers catch a glimpse of reality. If you want to steal any substantial number of them away, and hold onto them, you are going to have to provide substantially better value. A bit better product or a slightly lower price will not cut it.

As an interloper, you don't even get a seat at the market share poker table without superior customer value.

Some of the biggest marketing fiascos on record happened to companies that didn't understand this simple point. They thought they could take share by being new, or cute, or as good as the established players in the industry. They turned out to be wrong, big-time.

In 1979, Anheuser-Busch started Eagle Snacks to compete against Frito-Lay. What could be more natural than combining the distribution and sales of beer and salty snacks? The only problem was that the company forgot to build a value advantage into its new products. They weren't cheaper, they weren't better, and they certainly weren't fresher than Frito-Lay's direct-to-store products. What's more, A-B's incursion awakened a sleeping giant. Frito responded with a blizzard of new products as well as quality upgrades and price cuts on existing products. A-B's share of the snack market never topped 6 percent while Frito's increased from 40 percent to 50 percent. After seventeen years of losses, A-B put the Eagle brand to rest and sold its plants to— who else?—Frito-Lay.

Who remembers Petopia, the online retailer with the cute sock puppet as a pitch-dog? What was its superior value proposition? Don't know? Neither did Petopia. That situation reoccurred with countless other dot-bomb retailers who blazed across the sky burning bushels of venture capital money until they flamed out and fell back to a hard reality.

Then there was Netscape. The company's leaders exhausted themselves complaining about Microsoft's unfair marketing tactics. Meanwhile, they failed to improve upon their product for almost two years. They fell behind in the race for better value, for no reason other than inattention, and, as a result, market share slipped away, and they disappeared from view. Microsoft didn't bury Netscape. Netscape buried Netscape.

Given that superior value is essential to share gain, how do you go about achieving that superiority? Some guidance in that regard can be found in *The Discipline of Market Leaders,* the book I wrote with Fred Wiersema.

The first rule on the road to superior value, we argued, is to determine which of the three value disciplines you intend to stand out in. Do you want to focus on operational excellence to deliver lower total cost to customers, superior product quality, or customer intimacy? There's no way you can truly excel in more than one discipline at a time.

Once you have made your choice, there are three more rules to follow. You must redesign your company's operating model to conform with that discipline to achieve peak results. You must make certain that your company is performing at industry-average levels on the other two disciplines. And you must commit your company to an ironclad policy of improving its chosen value proposition year after year after year.

Historically, significant share gain comes about in two ways. The first and more common story stars a company that has devised a unique operating model capable of delivering superior customer value. The company proceeds to steal major market share from entrenched competitors, who defend rather than emulate; the company dominates the market, and the entrenched businesses die away.

This story has been repeated countless times, starring such retail category killers as Toys "R" Us, Wal-Mart, Staples, Best Buy, Starbucks, and Jiffy Lube. It can be seen playing out in systems integration, where Infosys, Satyam, Tata, and Wipro, four India-based companies, are commoditizing the application programming industry with a new low-cost, high-quality operating model and stealing significant market share from the likes of Accenture, IBM, and EDS. Capital One and MBNA have had similar success in the credit card industry.

But too often, businesses that achieve huge value advantages are unable or unwilling to abide by the fourth rule: commit to better value every year. Toys "R" Us , for example, initially had an easy time stealing market share from mom-and-pop toy retailers and inefficient mall-based toy chains, but now faces a life-threatening challenge from Wal-Mart. Jiffy Lube is facing the same situation. Its "next-generation" advantage has been matched by competitors that have rushed to meet its standard of value performance.

So wrapped up in their pursuit of market share, so enamored with their own success, these companies failed to recognize that they should have been engaged in a marathon, not a sprint—that today's value leadership is merely threshold value tomorrow.

The second kind of story, much rarer, is of an established business in a stable industry that builds its entire market share growth strategy on the fourth rule of value leadership. It improves customer value, year after year, faster than its competition, without ever declaring any "next-generation" advantage.

These are the turtles, not the hares. It is the story of Airbus and its thirty-year assault on Boeing's customer base. It is the story of BMW and its steady growth of market share in the North American luxury-car market. It is the story of Electronic Arts in the video game software marketplace, of Johnson & Johnson in skin care, and of Nokia in mobile telephones. Each of these companies has steadily grown market share using a very simple formula: improve customer value, year in and year out, faster than the competition, and you'll set a winning pace.

THE SECOND DISCIPLINE · 131

We are all familiar with the startling effects of compound arithmetic, illustrated by the old fable of the wise man who asked that the king give him just one grain of rice on the first square of a chess board and double the number of grains on each of the next sixty-three squares. Consistent improvements in customer value have that same compound effect. Customer value in many industries is increasing at about 3 or 4 percent per year. A company that doubles that rate of improvement will open up a 20 percent value advantage in about five years. That is a dominating advantage that would prove irresistible to customers in most markets.

To produce better value every year, a company must create and maintain a powerful innovation engine within its chosen value discipline. In the pages ahead, I suggest strategies for developing that engine. First though, a general observation.

To some degree, nothing you do to drive better value will be truly unique. That's because virtually every company is busily trying to copy best practices from leading-edge companies so that it can at least maintain threshold performance. For example, Dell's and Wal-Mart's supply-chain integration improvements are being emulated by hundreds of companies, not to become operationally excellent, but simply to meet a rising standard of operational competence. For you to gain a level of excellence that can win you share gain, you must transcend those efforts with pioneering innovations of your own.

Now, let's consider the ways to pursue innovation within the three value disciplines. In the case of *operational excellence,* you will want to look at three areas: supply-chain integration, customer-service processes, and the low-cost procurement of labor, assets, and supplies. Mobil's Speedpass is a good example of pioneering work to simplify and streamline a customer-service process. Infosys's sourcing of systems integrators from low-cost countries such as India, China, and the Philippines was a pioneering approach to labor procurement. easyJet's new discount jets will have only one bathroom but four extra seats because the company figured, correctly, that there would be less demand for facilities if passengers were charged for their beverages—a small example of how an organization focused on operational excellence has innovated to realize higher asset utilization.

For companies intent upon innovations in *product leadership,* the emphasis should be upon technology, be it the hard tech of industrial organizations or the soft tech of the financial world. As best-selling author and Harvard Business School professor Clay Christensen has observed, the most difficult decision these innovators must make is when to shift to the next generation of technology. There are countless examples of once-glorious product leaders such as Digital Equipment or U.S. Surgical that overstayed their dependence on old technology and perished. Product-leader companies must also pioneer in compressing the cycle time from product concept to peak revenue. Capital One, for example, has built the ability to rapidly identify, prototype, and test product innovations using its formidable information skills. The company claims to have run forty-five thousand such product tests in 2001 alone. Nowhere does the old phrase "Time is money" have greater import than among product leaders.

Businesses that pursue *customer intimacy* focus their innovation efforts on deepening and broadening their problem-solving expertise. Why? Because customers only buy total solutions from suppliers with know-how that exceeds their own. The problem is, every time a customer-intimate company delivers a total solution, it transfers some of its unique knowledge to the client, depreciating its uniqueness at a rapid rate. Hence the need for constant renewal of expertise. Fortunately, the experience of serving a range of customers provides the learning base for this renewal. In a Robin Hood tradition dear to the heart of management consultants, customer-intimate companies steal from their smarter customers, sanitize and generalize the insights, and transfer that knowledge to their other customers. That is what UPS's logistics arm does as it evolves a family of services to meet the ever more complex supply-chain needs of its customers.

The second area of innovation for customer-intimate companies is in managing the risks involved in achieving results for customers. Over time, many of their customer relationships shift to pay-for-performance, whereby a company contracts for a share of the results that it obtains on behalf of its customers. Convergys in billing and customer care, Exult in human resource outsourcing, and Johnson Controls in building management have created innovative risk-sharing contracts with customers that have come about because of their growing capacity to manage results.

The businesses that succeed in winning customers away from their rivals know how to innovate in their chosen value disciplines. These are the companies that establish best practices for others to adopt or emulate—and maintain that status from one year to the next. Their ability to continuously create better value starts with a commitment to innovation—a commitment that is buried deep within their organizations.

At the time of Sam Walton's passing, many a pundit declared that Wal-Mart was finished as a vibrant and feared competitor. They were proven wrong. How many analysts think that GE cannot continue its ascent without Jack Welch at the helm? Most, judging by the share price, but they too will be proven wrong.

At both companies, there is a mandate for customer-value innovation that permeates strategy and culture. Both organizations have developed a talent pool that is skilled, experienced, and motivated to create new operating-model innovations. And both corporations have an explicit process for managing operating-model innovation.

How many companies do you know that are willing or able to give their customers explicit commitments to value improvement? That's what Wal-Mart's rollbacks have done, creating in customers an expectation that prices will be permanently lower on many items the next time they shop at the store. It's what GE has done by budgeting 5 to 7 percent productivity improvements into every year's plan. It is a nonnegotiable expectation that all units of the company will find those productivity gains by improving their operating-model design. It's what Dell has done by declaring that it will cut another $1 billion from operating costs as it doubles its business in the next five years.

Along with commitment, your company must take care of the basics. You have to amass the skills, develop the experience, and provide the motivation for people to identify, create, and implement the required operating-model innovations. This is line-management work, which is why expert talent developers such as Wal-Mart, GE, and Dell place it on every line manager's career development path.

Who in your company should be primarily responsible for customer-value innovation? The top marketing people don't control the key levers. The head of manufacturing does affect costs and quality, but is consumed with operating issues.

The truth is that customer-value innovation cuts across all the functions of a business. It should be the responsibility of the entire management team. Typically, that means no one is in charge or the business-unit leader must take on the task, though rarely does such a person have the time to focus on this issue. That's why we're seeing a new seat at the table of many senior management teams, reserved for—you guessed it—the head of value innovation.

Buy Market Share Outright

There's another way to play the market share game. Rather than trying to woo away a competitor's customers, you can simply acquire the competitor—lock, stock, and customers.

There are two approaches to that strategy. You can practice the roll-up technique, rapidly buying up companies in a fragmented industry to create a large enterprise. That's what John Ledecky did when he grew U.S. Office Products to $4 billion in revenue before it all came crashing down. In the second approach, you buy a rival, fully integrate its customer base into your own operations, eliminate all vestiges of the acquired company, and thereby gather in new customers at a rock-bottom cost. That's the right approach.

The problem with U.S. Office Products and so many other roll-ups is that they are eventually revealed to be nothing more than large-scale Ponzi schemes. The company pays for its acquisitions by issuing new stock, which for a while rises in value because of the boost in growth that each acquisition creates. More acquisitions are made, more growth is achieved, and the stock price rises even further. What could be better?

Inevitably, this logic yields to an ugly reality. The roll-up company can't achieve economies of scale, either because it doesn't have a plan or because it's so busy absorbing new acquisitions that it has have no time to integrate them. What's more, all that buying activity leads sellers to demand a price premium, so the acquisitions get more and more expensive. The stock is eventually recognized for what it is—paper—and its value falls to earth, leaving investors in wreck and ruin. Even sophisticated investors have been caught. The prestigious private-equity firm, Clayton, Dubelier & Rice, invested $270 million in U.S. Office Products in 1998 for a 25 percent stake, and by 2001 the business was bankrupt.

Acquisition of market share makes great sense when three conditions obtain: there is no customer-acquisition premium; the operating model into which the acquired organization will be absorbed is well established; and the management team has the capacity to integrate the newcomer quickly. Let's take each in turn.

Price Premium. Every acquisition requires a price premium above the established value of the business, as an inducement to sell. The important calculation for the acquirer is whether the net cost per acquired customer is less than the cost of stealing those customers by going door to door. First Data Corporation, for example, acquires merchant accounts through its bank alliances for about $900 per merchant, which is less than its internal costs of customer acquisition, so market share gain through acquisition makes a lot of sense.

If you listen to investment bankers, they will tell you that as long as the cost per customer is less than the lifetime value of the customer, then you've gotten a good deal. But why pay more than your best alternative, which is to acquire the customers directly through your own means?

In the cable television business, acquisitions of cable operators used to cost about $1,000 per subscriber until AT&T upped the ante. The company paid more than $4,500 per subscriber for its last acquisitions, far above the cost of organic acquisition. DIRECTV is spending only $540 to gain a cable customer organically. AT&T's overpayment was a significant reason why Mike Armstrong's grand strategy failed and why the cable unit was merged with Comcast in November 2002.

Operating Model. The second condition for successfully buying market share is that the operating model into which the acquired company will be absorbed is robust. This growth strategy is about acquiring new customers, not new operating models. This is not a marriage of equals. It is a plan to acquire, dismember, and consume your competitor. Acquired customers are retained, acquired employees are retrained, acquired assets are redeployed, but acquired processes are to be destroyed and replaced with the business processes of the acquirer. In an ideal market share acquisition, when you're done there shouldn't be a shred of evidence that the old company ever existed.

In many acquisitions, such a strategy would be lunacy. Some of the differences in how an acquired company operates—different customer segment, different value proposition, different operating model pro-cesses—are too valuable to jettison. You may want to go ahead with the deal, but don't delude yourself that it's a market share acquisition. When a buy-out serves different segments of the marketplace that have different value demands, it can position your company in an-other part of the market, a move that I will discuss in the next chap-ter. But it doesn't meet the requirements of a share-gain buy.

Integration. The third condition for successful market share acquisi-tion is that management knows how to integrate quickly.

One of the great examples of superb acquisition integration was Columbia/HCA under Richard Scott's leadership. While much re-mains misunderstood about the Medicaid billing scandal that placed the company in turmoil, it is very clear that Scott created an integra-tion machine. During his tenure, Columbia/HCA acquired and inte-grated more than two hundred hospitals into an efficient and streamlined operating model. The keys were detailed planning and a robust operating model.

After a letter of intent had been signed and before the closing of the acquisition, Scott had a team of acquisition experts create a detailed hundred-day integration blueprint. It focused on transforming all of the business procedures of the hospital—procurement, real estate, per-sonnel, marketing, and, yes, billing practices—to Columbia/HCA's for-midable operating model. Medical practices were largely left alone. The hundred-day plan was prenegotiated with the acquired management team, right down to decisions about personnel. There were no surprises and every move was committed to a schedule. The expectation and the result was that one hundred days after the closing of the acquisition, that hospital was fully integrated into the Columbia/HCA system. The integration was highly disruptive to employees and suppliers, but it couldn't be disruptive to patients and insurers. It worked because of careful planning and fast execution—slow trigger, fast bullet.

By way of contrast, consider John McCoy of Bank One of Ohio. McCoy took over the bank that his father and grandfather had run and soon gained a reputation as a great acquirer. He bought banks in Texas, Arizona, Colorado, Illinois, and other parts of the country long before bank consolidation was a pervasive trend. Part of McCoy's success as an acquirer was what he called the "Uncommon Partnership," which meant, in practical terms, "If I buy you, I won't integrate you. You can still run your own bank." By 1995, Bank One had more than seventy different management teams, seventy different boards of directors, and a cost structure to prove it. By failing to speed the integration of its acquisitions, Bank One was unable to achieve the economies of scale that were within its grasp.

The acquisition of a competitor offers all sorts of potential advantages, but they cannot be truly realized unless the newcomer is integrated into your company. As long as the two of you are run as separate organizations, you aren't, for example, going to capture the cost savings the combined operation could provide. Instead, you will have the fixed expenses of two entities making their separate purchases, following their own longtime strategies, and living within their individual cultures. Fast integration avoids organizational clutter and complexity, the kind of two-kingdom arrangement where decisions are held up by a double dose of bureaucracy and execution is hostage to political in-fighting. By combining forces, you simply create a more powerful competitor and realize the benefits of greater market share.

Before signing off on acquisitions, I should note in passing the importance of capital structure and accounting methodology. There is no room to do justice to this large topic, but one important point must be made. When a company uses cash that it has generated, from either earnings or borrowings, to make an acquisition, that organization is providing growth for every shareholder. But when a company issues more of its own stock to make an acquisition or sells stock to others to raise cash for an acquisition, it may very well not be providing growth for every shareholder. After all, if two companies pool their interests and their shareholders to create one larger entity, is that growth? From a competitive perspective, yes, because the new entity has greater market share and presumably is a more formidable competitor. But from a shareholder perspective, all that has happened is that the pie has gotten bigger, but the investor's share has become proportionately smaller.

That's why Warren Buffett is emphatic that his Berkshire Hathaway will not pay for acquisitions with new shares of Berkshire. Buffett likes to pay cash that he has generated from earnings.

You have decided, despite the perils noted above, to follow the second growth discipline, devoting your company's resources, human and financial, to raiding your competitors' customer base. There are two basic ways you can go. You can seek to overcome the advantages that incumbency gives your rivals and directly challenge them on the basis of superior product, price, or service value. Or you can go whole hog and simply buy market share by buying your competitors. Each of the strategies has its proponents—and pitfalls.

I'd like to end this chapter where it began, with Airbus, and its mastery of the strategies required to achieve market share gain.

To start with, Airbus challenged its rivals on the basis of its superior product and service. It drove customer value improvements through superior product design. It understood what its airliner clients wanted—lowest operating costs and highest passenger comfort—and provided them on a level its competitors could not match.

The list of Airbus's product firsts is long. It was the first to produce a twin-engine, twin-aisle airliner. It was the first to reconfigure cockpit instrumentation so that a two-person crew could pilot a twin-aisle airplane. It was the first to introduce drag-reducing wingtips and fly-by-wire flight control systems. And, importantly, it was the first to introduce cross-crew qualification, so that pilots only had to be trained on the *differences* from one model to the next, lowering training costs and increasing crew productivity. Its next first? A four-aisle, twin-deck behemoth that will carry more than six hundred passengers, the A380.

Airbus has also been able to challenge its rivals' incumbent advantages. Its market is fairly efficient and responsive to a better value proposition. Potential customers are well known, and information about them easy to come by, for example, blunting that incumbent advantage. The company initially had a hard time getting serious consideration from North American airlines, but the receipt of a large order from Eastern Airlines in 1978 broke that barrier forever. Boeing cooperated by making it just as expensive to switch to another model or version of a Boeing airplane as it was to switch to those of a competitor, so carriers were accustomed to flying planes from a variety of manufacturers.

Indeed, it takes two parties to create a big shift in market share. In this case, Boeing was the compliant party. Its long and proud legacy in the airliner business had become more of a liability than an asset. Stubborn and burdened by old thinking, it was dismissive of Airbus's capabilities. In the end, the buck stops with senior management.

The second strategy, acquisition, was not a factor in the triumph of Airbus, but it can be a legitimate alternative to organic growth—assuming you follow the caveats listed above.

In fact, whichever strategy you choose to effect a market share gain, you should always be aware of the dangers of this discipline. Recognize that it's a lot easier to get hurt by a market share slide than it is to create a market share surge. And always consider the other parts of the growth portfolio, which may offer an easier and less costly way to grow.

One such alternative is coming up in the next chapter. It explains how you can go about growing by just showing up where growth is going to happen.

6

The Third Discipline: Show Up
Where Growth Is Going to Happen

Here's a riddle: how can you lose market share in every segment in which you do business, yet grow faster than your competitors? Give up? Here's the answer: you just need to lose share slowly in a big, fast-growing market segment that you dominate. That way, you'll grow quickly, even though you're losing share. Your competitors need to dominate all the segments that aren't growing. That way, they'll grow slowly, even though they're gaining share. It's all about market position.

That's basically what happened to Ford, GM, and Chrysler during the mid-nineties. While Asian manufacturers were eating into Detroit's share of the middle and bottom segments of the car market, and European and Asian rivals were dining on the luxury segment, the Big Three were selling a growing number of sport-utility vehicles (SUVs) and pickup trucks—segments that they dominated and that were growing quickly at the expense of auto sales. In fact, they were growing so rapidly that the unit growth more than made up for the companies' market share losses in every segment.

From 1992 to 1996, domestic car sales grew a total of only 3.5 percent and the Big Three's share of the market dropped about 1.5 points to 65.3 percent. Light truck sales, meanwhile, grew 43 percent, fueled by an 89 percent increase in SUV sales. Detroit manufacturers dominated the light truck segment with an 86.7 percent share and they managed to lose only a small fraction of their light truck share from 1992 to 1996. Because they lost market share more slowly in the part of the market that was growing the fastest, incredibly, they grew their overall market share during this period by almost 1 point, to 74.6 percent of the total domestic market.

But nothing lasts forever. By 1996, the Japanese and Europeans began turning out SUVs that could compete with Detroit's versions, and the overseas automakers have since corralled more than one third of that market while the segment's growth rate has been cut in half. As a result, the Big Three has lost more than 10 percent of the overall market since 1996.

The moral of the story is simple: if the hardest way to grow is by stealing market share from your competitors, the easiest is to stake out a strong position in a part of your market that is growing and ascend with the rising tide. In other words, shift your market mix toward the fastest-growing segments.

The key to successful market positioning is to identify and invade the new hot spots before your competitors, and there's no shortage of potential spots to monitor. Few markets are homogeneous. Even the markets for commodity products, such as steel, crude oil, and water, have their distinct areas—segments that offer different products to a different set of customers, that use different distribution channels, and that post different growth rates.

And when you make your move into a growing market segment, you should invade in force. It's a no-brainer: the stronger your position in a booming market segment, the larger your gain. If you have zero percent of a segment growing at 100 percent a year, you get zero. If you can get in on the ground floor, and build a decent share position, then 100 percent market growth will automatically double your business every year.

Market positioning presents two basic challenges: you have to spot a growth segment, and you then have to seize and hold onto a substantial chunk of the action. In this chapter, my focus is on the first challenge, since the mechanics of winning market share were covered in the previous chapter. There are, however, some interesting differences in the competitive circumstances.

If you already have a position, albeit small, in a growth segment of your market, you have the advantages of incumbency—not only with your customers in that segment but with those in your other segments. So do your rivals.

But since the real growth in the segment, generally, will be in the number of newly arriving, unaffiliated customers, the advantages of incumbency loom small. So much for the first strategy of share gain. The third strategy, buy market share by acquiring competitors, is irrelevant since no one yet has a substantial customer base.

In fact, most of your energies will have to be spent following the second strategy: deliver far better value. In this case, though, superior value will not be needed so much to blunt incumbent advantages as to corral discriminating newcomers, who are making active purchase decisions. The trick is to position yourself with top value before a segment enters into its fastest growth period so you can gain a maximum market share with a minimum of struggle.

Spot the Growth Plays Early

In the pages to come, then, I concentrate on spotting growth plays early, not on what to do after they are spotted. Immediately ahead, I list three leading indicators of changes that hint at the presence of new fast-growth market segments. Later on, I discuss how you can organize your company to search out these segments. The three indicators are:

- Shifts in buying criteria. Those who last week bought on price, say, now only care about product quality, or vice versa.

- Leaps in customer value. Product or service innovations are pulling new customers into a long-dormant segment.
- Trends in demographics. Population trends are producing more potential customers for a given market.

Before discussing these shifts in detail, I have two caveats. The first: in assessing the growth potential of a market segment, you should examine its gross profits. Take the segment's sales revenue, subtract the cost of raw materials and production, and you will have a direct measure of the gross profit, the premium customers are willing to pay for goods or services. If that premium is rising, it usually means that the customer base is rising or that existing customers are buying more. A rise in total gross profit within a market segment should raise a flag in your organization: a market-positioning opportunity may be knocking. By the same token, a gross profit decline should signal a problem segment in the making. In either case, if you rely simply on measures such as revenue, you are likely to misjudge. Markets with declining gross margins, for example, may be increasing revenue much faster than they are growing gross profits.

The second caveat: this chapter is solely dedicated to anticipating which segments of your market are going to grow the fastest and positioning your enterprise there to get the biggest boost from market growth. It is not about finding growth opportunities in an adjacent market or in another industry, both of which are treated in later chapters. The distinction is important because a common operating model, with some variation, can serve different market segments. Market positioning may require a change in emphasis, but it does not require the kind of major business shifts necessary to penetrate an entirely new market.

Now, let's examine the three positioning indicators.

Shifts in Buying Criteria

When customers shift their value demands, they kick-start new growth segments. Your task: recognize the signs that customers are on the move; figure out where they're headed; then plant yourself at their destination and reap substantial growth rewards.

The problem with spotting shifts in buying criteria is that there are so many of them. Customers are constantly changing. Some of the shifts are no more than a temporary blip, making not a dent in the market segment; others are long-term and spark fundamental segment change. Sometimes, customer shifts are actually contradictory. Is there a trend toward healthier food and healthier lifestyles? Of course, but what about the trends toward obesity and passive entertainment?

It would make our lives easier if these customer shifts moved in a predictable manner. In fact, it has often been conjectured that as markets mature, customers tend to switch from a desire for the best product to a desire for the best total solution and finally end up chasing the best price.

But there is ample evidence that the conjecture has it wrong, that customers can shift *from* any dimension *to* any dimension of value.

To familiarize you with the forms these shifts can take, here are some examples of customers' buying criteria on the move.

From "Best Healthcare" (Product) to "Most Cost-Effective Healthcare" (Price). In the early 1990s, healthcare costs were spiraling upward at three times the rate of inflation. General Motors was complaining loudly to any lawmaker who would listen that employee healthcare made up more of the cost of a Chevy than did steel. Bill Clinton ran on a platform of healthcare reform and after the election put his wife, Hillary, in charge of restructuring the entire industry. The effort failed, but it catalyzed a major shift in corporate healthcare buying. The winners were efficient hospital chains, such as HCA and HealthSouth, which recognized that managed care would open up new segments of the hospital industry. The losers were local and regional hospitals that didn't have the scale to become efficient. Corporate customers and their proxies, the insurance companies, had changed their priorities and their criteria.

From "Best Food Products" (Product) to "Best Meal for My Schedule" (Total Solution). Traditional grocery sales are inching upward at a rate of 2.5 percent annually. Right next door, in outside-the-home dining and in heat-'n'-eat packaged meals, are market segments growing at much faster rates. In which segments would you rather be?

As has become so evident in recent years, consumers are eating out more often and substituting "grazing" for traditional family meals. The latter-day Ozzie and Harriet and their kids eat their food on the go—in the car, at the mall, in the street. And those who still want to eat at home have less time to cook during the day. The rising number of single adults, working women, and senior citizens with more disposable income than ever before means that more people are willing to pay for the convenience of takeout food and partially or fully prepared meals. In 1986, fully half of all meals in the United States were prepared and eaten at home. Today, that is true of less than one third of our meals. That's a customer criteria shift of major proportions.

From "Best Wealth Manager" (Total Solution) to "Best Investment" (Product). It's no secret that full-service brokerage firms, such as Merrill Lynch and UBS PaineWebber, have been losing retail customers to mutual-fund providers such as Fidelity and Janus for years. Customers sold on mutual funds as an investment decided that all the comforts of the full-service firms could not make up for the less-than-impressive track records of their internally managed funds. Customer criteria switched from overall to particular, from total solution to product. Merrill Lynch and UBS PaineWebber responded by offering customers outside, name-brand mutual funds, slowing the client drain but not stopping it.

From "Best Wealth Manager" (Total Solution) to "Lowest-Fee Investing" (Price). On another front, the full-service brokers have fallen victim to a major shift in customers' priorities. More and more investors have been willing to forgo the advice—and high trading fees—of the traditional brokers on their way to signing on with Schwab, Vanguard, and the cut-rate e-traders. No way could the full-service firms, stuck with astronomical cost structures, hold onto or win back the fast-growing, price-sensitive investor segments.

From "Best Price on a Pickup" (Price) to "Best Pickup Design on the Road" (Product). Pickup trucks have been around for a long, long time, but as utilitarian vehicles. In 1994, Chrysler sparked a revolution in pickup design by answering the question, "Why can't a pickup be more like a car?" Suddenly, customers whose buying decisions had been based on cost were exposed to pickups that were so sleek and comfortable they could double as cars. Ford and GM quickly came up with their own designs, and this new–old market segment boomed. Pickups today have the highest brand-repurchase rate of any category of vehicles.

To win in market segments that are growing because of a shift in customer buying criteria, you need to place your bets on the value destination to which customers are migrating. In the following pages, I examine two more indicators of market segment growth. Perhaps the single most important reason for a change in the growth rate of a market segment is the rapid acceleration of a dimension of value fueled by operating model innovation. A sea change in the composition or characteristics of the consumer population can also be a major catalyst.

Leaps in Customer Value

When value rises greatly in a market segment, customers start rushing in, creating a market-positioning opportunity. That value shift is a signal for you to pay attention and possibly jump into the segment. Happily, you won't have to top competitors' value offerings; just staying with the pack will do the trick and earn you a decent share of the growing market.

Most major value innovations are not new to the world, just new to your market. The critical judgment you have to make is about the timing and probability of a successful transfer of the innovation to your market. Dell's direct-selling, build-to-order operating model, for example, has been around for a long time. It is now starting to ignite growth in segments of the credit card and mobile phone markets where customers are eager to buy fully personalized products. Advanta's hottest-selling business credit card allows customers to choose their billing date and affinity and even place their company name on the card—a chip off the old Dell value innovation.

Leaps in customer value are created by three forms of innovation: technology breakthroughs, process breakthroughs, and expertise breakthroughs.

Technology Breakthroughs. If you seek market-positioning candidates, you should, first and foremost, examine all conceivably relevant technical advances through the lens of your market. The wireless phone segment within the larger telephone equipment industry is a classic example of invention fueling segment growth. While traditional phone equipment has grown only marginally over the past five years, the wireless segment has exploded. About four hundred million wireless phones were sold worldwide in 2002, accounting for $60 billion in revenues and $18 billion in gross profits. That's ten times the number sold in 1995—a compound annual growth rate of 40 percent.

Few traditional telephone manufacturers were able to reposition themselves successfully for the wireless market, even though the technology was well within their grasp. Their operating models were not geared to cope with the rigors of intense product leadership competition. Siemens, a traditional phone maker, had greater flexibility. Its wireless operations had sales of $5 billion in 2002, generating more than $1.5 billion in gross profits.

A second example of segment growth driven by technological innovation can be found in the drug industry. That happened when the pharmaceutical industry focused its attention on developing treatments for a whole new set of problems. Among them: Minoxidil, to repair hair loss; Viagra, for enhanced sexual performance; and Retin-A, to reduce age lines in skin. The drug labs are now chasing products to enhance memory, increase physical stamina, and, the big prize, safely reduce weight. In each case, the technological breakthroughs were signs that a new growth market was in the works, though it would be a while before companies other than the patent-holding organization could enter the fray.

Process Breakthroughs. Rapid improvements in customer value, specifically in price and convenience, become possible with process innovation. The discount airline segment within the larger airline industry offers an outstanding example. Southwest, JetBlue, Ryanair, and easyJet are four leading examples of startups that moved quickly to exploit a new segment of the airline industry and have shown consistent double-digit growth by being in the right segment at the right time. Surprisingly, every traditional airline that tried to jump into this lucrative segment has failed. KLM Dutch Airlines is just the latest to accept defeat, selling its discount division to Ireland's Ryanair. It's an indication that the cost-heavy traditional airlines' operating models just can't fly in the discount segment.

Process breakthroughs have also fueled fast-growing segments in the retail market. The Target chain is a prime example. While other discounters based their customer appeal almost entirely on price, Target devised a unique, oxymoronic strategy: it would be an upscale discounter. To succeed, the company would have to develop the processes to deliver a shopping experience that was not only easy on the pocketbook but also pleasant and convenient. As opposed to the typical discounter, Target stores would have to be clean and tidy, the wares attractively displayed, the aisles wide, the salespeople courteous and efficient, the checkout speedy. The chain has been a remarkable success, owing in large part to its innovative processes. Front-line people were trained to treat customers as guests and given solid reasons to enjoy their work, such as especially generous benefits and an egalitarian culture in which everyone in the organization is on a first-name basis and wears the company uniform of red shirt and khaki pants. World-famous designers were sold on producing low-priced lines of their products exclusively for Target, giving the stores a special panache. In one area after another, the company created breakthrough processes that opened up a new retail growth segment.

Expertise Breakthroughs. You can also look for growth segments wherever companies are creating deep expertise in solving their clients' problems and delivering meaningful results. In the business-services marketplace, for example, hot new segments have come to the fore based on the management of business processes in human resources, customer service, and finance. Payroll processing is perhaps the granddaddy of business-process management. So far fewer than 20 percent of all companies have outsourced payroll management, but that's been enough to fuel 18 percent market growth, which has powered ADP and Paychex to double-digit growth.

The demand for outside process expertise has been sparked by a widespread trend among companies to reduce the complexity of their operations and focus their energies on their core concerns. More and more, they are outsourcing secondary processes to specialists. Convergys saw the opportunity for entering the fast-growth customer-service management segment when the company was part of Cincinnati Bell. It broke away from the old phone company and has doubled its business in five years' time by taking over billing and customer call centers for its telephone company clients.

Life cycle management of capital goods as diverse as power plants and locomotives is another set of segments where new expertise has powered value innovation and growth. These service businesses are now among the fastest-growing segments in their industrial-products markets as many companies discover that the real gross profit dollars are to be found in expertise-based services rather than product sales. That's why Rockwell Automation, Boeing, and a host of other companies are using acquisitions and organic efforts to take new market positions in services. It's a page right out of GE's playbook.

Trends in Demographics

When large numbers of people experience a major change in their lives, you should pay attention. It means that your marketplace is probably going to feel the effects. More to the point, it means that market-positioning opportunities are knocking.

Not that population changes are so hard to spot—after all, they take place over years, if not decades. The trick is to determine what impact they will have on your bailiwick, how to go about taking advantage of the resulting growth segments—and when to jump in. Generally speaking, sooner is better.

Demographic shifts come in three basic areas: life stages, geography, and economics. Let's take a look at them one by one.

Life Stages. The evolution of the baby-boomer generation is perhaps the best-known example of how population growth can affect the prospects of market segments. As the boomers have passed from one life stage to the next, like a clinched pig through a python, they have created booms and busts in almost every market segment they enter and leave. Now that boomers are approaching sixty years of age, they are poised to fuel major growth in all manner of retirement services, from financial planning to nursing homes, just as they earlier drove growth in everything from consumer debt to pediatric care.

Geography. The population of any given area of the world ebbs and flows with the tides of popular taste, the availability of work, and the nation's immigration policies. In the United States, the industrial Midwest, with its high wages and outmoded infrastructure, lost business and workforce to the industrializing South after World War II. Over the past two decades, there has been a steady population shift from the rest of the country to the desert Southwest.

Such migrations affect everything in their path, from the price of real estate to demand for automobiles, appliances, utilities, and mortgages. For example, from 2000 through 2002, residential construction was flat in the Northeast but grew at better than 6 percent in the Southwest. Where would you rather position your residential-construction business if you're looking for growth? The same question can be asked if you sell carpets, furniture, or anything else that goes into those houses.

Economics. The opportunities for positioning your company in a growth market segment increase with the increasing wealth of your potential customer base. The traditionally low incomes of residents of developing countries, such as China and India, are poised to rise, in some cases dramatically, over the next decades. For a company such as Gillette, for example, the scenario plays out as follows: New business expansion in, say, China, leads to improvements in wages. The cost of a month's supply of disposable razors, expressed in minutes of labor, drops. The major barrier to purchase having been removed, sales rise rapidly.

Western Union faces a different opportunity with the improved economic status of its immigrant customers, who rely on the company for efficient transfer of funds back to their homelands. Now, as their incomes rise, their needs become more complex. There are a multitude of financial service segments, beyond money transfer, that will feel the impact of the economic progression of the immigrant workers. The strategy? Position the enterprise in some of the fastest-growing segments to enjoy the benefits of a rising tide.

Organize the Search

If market positioning is the easiest way to grow, then why do so few companies do it well? Why do we see the same organizations, year after year, competing in the same slow-growth, dead-end market segments?

Some companies regard their market position as a given and never bother to think twice about it. Others view the barriers to a change in market position as insurmountable. Sadly, most companies don't even know how much market segment growth contributes to their total growth.

To spot positioning opportunities and make the most of them, you need something few companies can claim: a systematic approach to managing the process. Repositioning needs to be a continuing operation that is built into the routine processes of management.

Consider the American International Group, the largest insurance company in the United States. Maurice Greenberg has run it for the past thirty-five years. His stewardship has been the stuff of legend: revenue and profits have grown at double-digit rates for most of the past decade to more than $65 billion in revenue and $7 billion in after-tax earnings.

Much of Greenberg's success owes to his uncanny ability to position his company early in the richest and most rewarding segments of the insurance market. AIG has a rigorous system of management that gives as much consideration to turning up promising new market positions as most organizations give to costs. It keeps a constant eye out for new forms of risk where it can innovate and grow. In 2002, for example, in conjunction with Equifax, AIG launched Internet identity theft coverage to protect consumers against electronic fraud.

Many forms of specialty casualty insurance are classic boom-and-bust market segments, chronically shifting from undersupply to oversupply and back again. Greenberg is a contrarian who leaps into segments just as his competitors are leaping out, frightened away by low premiums and high losses. He understands that as companies throw in the towel, the supply of insurance dries up, rates move upward, sometimes dramatically, and requirements on the customer tighten. That's why AIG launched a new set of directors' and officers' insurance products in November 2002, just as corporate scandals and impending lawsuits put a cloud over the whole market.

To walk in AIG's footsteps with your own system for identifying positioning opportunities, you need to become a student of your entire market, not just the part you occupy. If you don't understand the dynamics of every segment within your market, if you can't at any moment accurately predict the potential for growth in total gross profits of all of these segments, then you become a prisoner of your ignorance. Lacking well-understood options, you cannot take advantage of the repositioning possibilities.

Much of the data required to achieve that informed state will not be generated by your financial-reporting systems, and it usually can't be bought from a syndicated data service. It has to be pieced together using research, private and public information sources, and analytic detective work. Create an information base that encompasses past and current shifts in buying criteria, value innovation, and demographics. Gauge market segment size as well as current and forecast growth rates. It's a considerable task, but it can be done with a commitment of time and talent.

Now, armed with knowledge, you are ready to measure your company's existing market position against an "ideal" position in the highest-growth segments of the market. In effect, the comparison answers the question, "What growth rate is adverse market position costing me?" The gap between current and ideal growth in market position will guide you in tilting your market mix toward the higher-growth segments.

Every business unit must shoulder responsibility for achieving this goal. But that will only happen if you recognize and reward effective market-positioning efforts with the same enthusiasm as you recognize and reward market share gains.

Another organization that is actively managing its market position is United Auto Group (UAG). Founded by Marshall Cogan, the New York financier, the company was designed to be an automobile mega-dealer that would use its buying power to press carmakers for better prices and higher profits. But investors became disillusioned with the story, and by the time Roger Penske, the famous Indianapolis race car driver, bought a controlling interest in 1999, UAG had lost more than 80 percent of its value.

Penske came to the conclusion that there was more money to be made by partnering with manufacturers than by opposing them. Recognizing that the various segments of the auto-dealer business carried very different gross profits, he determined to reposition UAG toward segments with high margins and fast growth.

A few numbers suggest just how different the segments of the auto-dealership market can be. At UAG, new-car sales generated 60 percent of its $6.2 billion in 2001 revenue but only a third of the gross profits. That's because new-car sales carry only an 8 percent gross margin. By way of contrast, service and parts generate equal or greater gross profits on a sixth of the revenues. Parts has 31 percent profit margins, while service's margins are a mighty 65 percent. Customers see a lot more value in a dealer's service operation than in its sales department. Other segments that generate higher profits than new-car sales include body-shop work, financing, and the sale of insurance.

The sale of new cars, of course, was the catalyst that created demand for all the other services. But UAG was not doing a very good job of selling its other offerings to its new-car customers. Penske and his management team changed that by putting all their market segments under a managerial microscope, then shifting their mix of business toward higher-margin segments. For example, in 2001, they increased their revenues from financing by 17 percent per store while new-car sales grew at 10 percent. They now have a similar focus on higher-margin service work, where there is an even greater loss of opportunity because so many customers take their trade elsewhere.

Latecomers, Beware

Market positioning works best when it works early, for two main reasons. First, you benefit from entering a growing market segment in direct proportion to the share of the market you control. Second, and of greater importance, you can quietly build market share and refine operating model capabilities before the potential of the market segment is widely understood. Once fast growth in a segment is established and understood, competitors tenaciously defend their prize.

But what if you *are* late to a market segment, growth is in full boil, and you can't resist the opportunity that it presents? Simple words of advice: prepare for mortal combat. Remember, market share gain is the toughest, nastiest way to grow a company because your gain comes at someone else's expense. Two things need to happen simultaneously for a company to have any chance of success under these conditions. You have to deliver a value innovation that has a whopping impact, and you need to catch an established competitor asleep at the wheel. If you can enter the growth segment with superior customer value *and* have the good fortune to face a competitor who has taken the market for granted and allowed its value to erode, then, and only then, do you stand a good chance of success.

That's exactly what happened when the Japanese automobile manufacturers turned their attention to the luxury-car segment. German and American manufacturers were dismissive of Toyota's efforts, giving them the opportunity to enter the market with a powerful combination of product design and price. Within a year of launch, Toyota's flagship model was named the car of the year by the Motoring Press Association. The rest, as they say, is history.

Dead Enders—Get Out

For some industries, market repositioning is out of the question—they have just gone bad and stayed that way. Bananas, for instance, have been a bad business for forty years: quality, competition, and consumption have all increased, but bananas have been so commoditized that the wholesale price has actually dropped over that period from sixty-five cents a pound to eighteen cents. Since no one has found a way to transform the product with added value, returns on bananas continue to spiral down, with no remedy in sight.

Mining often seems highly attractive when players first sit down at the table. But mining hasn't earned a fair return on invested capital since the bad old days of inflation economies. Many mining companies, including Noranda, Phelps Dodge, and Inco, routinely trade at a discount to their book value. In fact, without inflation, there is no reason to be in the mining business.

Profits from mining depend mainly on just three factors: commodity prices, the quality of the ore, and operating efficiency. Prices fluctuate, but generally decline as new mines enter the industry, new operating economies add to capacity, and synthetic substitutes eat into the overall market. Ore quality declines as a mine ages, and improvements in efficiency require infusions of capital. But closing an old mine tends to be all but impossible because of prohibitive environmental costs.

In short, having anted up, a player in the mining business finds this is a poker game where you can't win, you can't break even, and you can't leave the game.

Given a bad business, here are some of your options:

Sell Out and Try Something Else. In 1987, when Jerry Tsai found himself stuck in a dead-end packaging market as chief executive of staid old American Can, he changed the name to Primerica, found a buyer for the manufacturing assets, and used the proceeds to buy Smith Barney, American Capital Management & Research, and A. L. Williams. The next year he merged with Travelers Insurance. Tsai's successor, Sanford Weill, completed the trifecta by merging Travelers with Citicorp and winding up as CEO of one of the world's largest and most dynamic financial institutions.

Industry Restructure. It is slow and painful, but if you can enlist your investment banks in the effort, this is a reliable way to clean out overcapacity and pave the way for healthy growth. In the chemical industry, low growth, heavy environmental costs, and crushing cyclicality have eroded returns for years, while government regulation makes it cheaper to continue operating an inefficient plant than to close it down. In fact, it costs less to buy an entire chemical company than to build a single new plant. These organizations actually have negative goodwill: the value of the business is less than the replacement cost of the hard assets. The industry has responded with a round of consolidation aimed at reducing its total capacity and easing the pressure on prices. Some analysts predict that when the carrousel finally stops, there will be only four survivors: Dow, DuPont, Bayer, and BASF.

Ingenuity. The best way to cope with a bad market, of course, is to find some corner of it that everyone else has overlooked or to find a business model so powerful that it transforms bad to good. Tatem & Associates is a small insurance agency in Terre Haute, Indiana. In 1991, it discovered the growth niche in a stagnant market: serving volunteer fire departments, which have unique insurance needs, given their volunteer workforce and the effect of fighting fires on the firefighters' life and health insurance. This agency built a regional practice and a dominating market share. It has found a pearl among the swine.

It also takes a high level of ingenuity to create a next-generation business model that actually exploits the problems no one else can solve. We make heroes of those who make that happen: Sam Walton, whose Wal-Mart is the one great business in a lousy industry; Michael Dell, whose Dell Computer continues to turn revenues and profits long after the personal computer market turned sour for everyone else; and Herb Kelleher, who built the puddle-jumping Southwest Airlines into a business whose market capitalization is bigger than the rest of the airline industry put together.

The good news is that, for the vast majority of businesses, the growth that comes with market positioning does not require such heroic efforts. You do need to have a firm comprehension of your market segments, and a weather eye on the signals that are or may soon be changing—the shifts in customer criteria, customer value, and demographics discussed above. The chances are good that the effort you make to follow this third discipline of market growth will be well rewarded.

There are, though, other disciplines in my growth portfolio. In the next chapter, I take up one of them—the possibility of your moving into markets that are close to, but not within, your own market.

7

The Fourth Discipline:
Invade Adjacent Markets

In May 2001, a six-hundred-pound gorilla named Microsoft burst upon the video game scene. At the Electronic Entertainment Expo in Los Angeles, the software giant announced its plan to release a state-of-the-art console, the Xbox.

Ken Kutaragi, president of Sony Computer Entertainment and the father of Sony's dominant PlayStation products, was not impressed. "Microsoft was finished even before it got started," he told a *Financial Times* reporter. "They have no games." In other words, the Xbox initiative was weak in precisely the area one might have expected it to be strongest.

As it turned out, Kutaragi was right in the short term—the Xbox has been racking up huge losses—but the game isn't over. Microsoft's entry is tied for second place in the market with longtime gamer Nintendo, and this gorilla has stamina.

The Sony–Microsoft battle illustrates many of the complexities and perils of seeking double-digit growth in an adjacent market, the fourth discipline of my growth portfolio. In this chapter, I describe the strategies that can yield success in adjacencies, showing how they have supported companies such as Sony and Johnson & Johnson and been badly managed by others such as AT&T. I also discuss the advantages, and disadvantages, of taking the acquisition route into an adjacent market.

First, though, let's define an adjacent market. Any given market has its own cost structures, competitors, customers, and requisite capabilities. Markets that don't differ significantly in terms of those four criteria are actually one market. Small variations in the criteria produce different market segments within the same market. If there are important similarities as well as large differences, these are separate but adjacent markets. If the business is too far afield, if costs, competitors, customers, and capabilities are all different, we're talking about entirely independent markets, requiring new lines of business—the subject of my next chapter.

For example, when Ken Kutaragi led Sony's march into video games in 1994, he understood that it was an adjacent market to Sony's core entertainment and consumer electronics businesses. It varied from the company's customary business with regard to at least three of the four criteria. Cost structures for hardware were similar to consumer electronics, but video gaming was primarily built on the economics of software, much like Sony's music business. Competitors were different, and the required operating model, while it relied heavily on Sony's existing capabilities, also required significant augmentation, especially in software development. There were differences enough to make video games a separate market, but similarities enough to make it familiar and thus adjacent.

For some fortunate companies, adjacency simply represents another opportunity to put their superior operating model to work in a new high-growth market. Essentially, that was why Sony jumped into video games, but many companies simply have little choice. Caught in a small or stagnant market, they are desperate for growth, and the fast-moving markets right next door represent necessity as well as opportunity.

Michael Dell is pushing his eponymous company into networking, storage, and services. Why? Because he sees that his traditional personal computer market is increasingly plagued by low growth, overcapacity, and irrational competition—the usual suspects found at the end-state of any industry. He understands that his company must seek new paths to growth, and, as we've seen, adjacencies such as networking are within sight.

Any company contemplating a move into an adjacency needs to answer three key questions:

1. Should you enter this market? That is, does it promise significant opportunities for long-term growth and profitability?

2. Can you win in this market? Do you have major advantages over your competitors?

3. Can you match the standards of competition in this market? Your strategic advantage will not hold if you fall behind competitors in the rest of your offering.

Let's look more closely, now, at Sony's experience in video games and see what kind of answers it found to those questions—and how they differed from Microsoft's answers.

Sony put its first toe in the market in 1991 when the company and Nintendo announced plans for a CD peripheral for Nintendo's sixteen-bit machine. Sony set about designing a prototype and developing several games, but, less than a year later, Nintendo bowed out of the agreement, apparently because it would have allowed Sony to reap the publishing profits from games that ran on the CD peripheral. Nintendo promptly set to work on a new peripheral with Philips, and Sony walked away angry.

Nintendo was an old hand in this market. The company began selling games and toys in 1963 and, by 1977, had developed its first home video game system; eight years later, it held 90 percent of the market for new video game consoles, powered in large measure by the Super Mario Brothers game.

Sega was a latecomer, but it caught up. That company's first consoles, released in 1985, were a flop, but its sixteen-bit Genesis system, out in 1988, was a generation ahead of Nintendo's machine. When EA Sports released the Madden Football video game two years later, the Genesis console took off. By 1994, with the help of its Sonic the Hedgehog game, Sega had captured 55 percent of the market for consoles.

At that point, the video game business seemed a questionable target for a company interested in adjacent-market growth. It was, to begin with, totally dominated by two entrenched companies that would do their best to keep another contender from gaining a foothold. Moreover, the sixteen-bit machines were reaching the end of their life cycle, the market appeared to be saturated at thirty million installed units, and revenues had flattened. In terms of the first of the questions that need to be answered before taking on an adjacency— should anyone want to enter this market?—many managers thought the answer was a resounding no.

Yet, several major corporations, including Panasonic and Philips as well as Sony, believed that a potential bonanza awaited the organization that could introduce a machine powerful enough to handle three-D graphics. The current sixteen-bit console was not up to the job of bringing the magic of Hollywood to the tiny video game screen. The problem was, the new machine would require entirely new programming tools and demand new game concepts. Pac Man and Tetris, though not dead, were relics of the past. In the race for the three-D prize and market dominance, industry analysts thought Sony was a long shot. David Cole, president of DFC Intelligence, an industry watcher, noted that "Traditional consumer-electronics manufacturers have yet to establish a viable model for making money from this industry." The "future leaders," he added, would be Nintendo and Sega because of their "software skills."

Sony begged to differ. The company believed that the game market was flat not because of any fundamental problem with demand but because of an absence of vision and marketing flair on the part of the market leaders. Video games were being sold to children as toys, while Sony envisioned them as an entertainment medium for adults, as well. The technology shift away from the sixteen-bit consoles, Sony believed, would destabilize the market and present a serious entry opportunity for a company that arrived early with a high-quality thirty-two-bit machine.

In the end, Sony concluded that the video game market was a prime adjacency prize with a probable double-digit growth rate. Now, the company was ready to move on to the second adjacent-market question: could it win in that market? Did Sony have major advantages that would enable it to unseat the market leaders?

There were two areas in which Sony thought it could outperform Nintendo and Sega. The first was clear and obvious: the company's formidable manufacturing expertise meant that it should be able to drive its delivered cost of consoles well below that of its competitors. If Sony then priced the consoles at or near cost, it would make it very expensive for Sega and Nintendo to gain market share. In the long term, the company hoped to ride the price-experience curve down to the point of selling consoles for less than $100. At that price, video game consoles could become as ubiquitous as television sets.

Sony's second key advantage was a strategy tailored to the inside-out economics of the video game business, where manufacturers traditionally made most of their money in software, not hardware. The consoles were sold for a small profit, but the real money was in the sale of homegrown video games and in collecting a license fee from independent developers whose games ran on their consoles. In its fleeting and unhappy 1991 experience with Nintendo, Sony had discovered that independent software developers felt abused by the console vendors. Until 1988, Nintendo had insisted that developers working on software for the company not work for its competitors. Sega wasn't any different. When it released a new machine in 1992, Sega denied developers access to several key graphical features of the machine, which the corporation was saving for its own programming efforts.

Lacking any serious expertise in game development, Sony would be almost totally dependent upon those independent developers. Its strategy for invading the video game business was to fully embrace the fast-growing developer community and make its members part of the Sony team. The company planned to put EA Sports, Activision, CapCom, Acclaim, and all the other independent software companies on an equal footing, treat them fairly, and together build successful businesses on a thirty-two-bit platform. Getting developers to devote themselves to games for a brand new, untested console would be a challenge, but nothing that Sony, with its considerable international prestige, could not handle.

The company would be aided by its experience in the recording industry, which had given Sony an understanding of the intricacies of licensing arrangements and third-party relationships. It would also be able to harness its consumer-electronics engineering skills to design a console that would be extremely easy to develop games on, which would help it become the machine of choice for developers.

Having satisfied itself that it did have the kind of potent advantages required to win in the adjacent video game market, Sony turned to the third adjacency question: did it have the skills and resources to at least hold its own in the other operating requirements of the game business?

There seemed little doubt that the company could match the standards of competition in marketing and distribution. Sony was a master at convincing consumers around the world to buy its electronic wares. To the degree that the game business broadened from toys to entertainment, Sony's existing expertise would be even more applicable. As to distribution, the venues where game consoles and software were sold, including mass merchants and electronics chains, were already customers for Sony's other products.

Convinced that it could compete successfully in the video game adjacency, Sony launched its PlayStation console in Japan in December 1994 and followed it with North American and European launches in September 1995. The company followed through on its strategy, and succeeded beyond all expectations, though its victory was owed, in part, to competitors' mistakes.

Sega, for example, launched its thirty-two-bit Saturn console several months before Sony's machine, but demanded a price of $400, even though Sony's PlayStation was soon out there selling for $300. When Sega finally cut its price to meet Sony's in January 1996, the PlayStation was outselling the Saturn four to one.

Sega's Saturn launch was further compromised when the company gave Electronics Boutique, Toys "R" Us, and Neo Star exclusive access to the product for a period of months. That naturally angered the rest of the retail community. Ever since, many outlets have refused to give Sega products shelf space equal to the amount allotted PlayStation.

The most significant mistake made by Sega, though, was to bring out Saturn too soon, without enough support from independent software producers. Caught off-guard, the developers had almost no software ready.

Nintendo stumbled in a different way. Having decided to skip thirty-two-bit machines and go straight to sixty-four-bit architecture, the company could not deliver its new consoles until Sony's PlayStation had been in the market for a full year. By then, Sony had sold 7.5 million PlayStations, and the momentum was still building.

Moreover, Nintendo's advanced architecture gave the company scant advantage over PlayStation since both could run the three-D graphics that every gamer sought. And Nintendo's avowed preference for proprietary software titles didn't inspire the independent developers to turn out much product for the N64—EA Sports, for one, chose not to develop a single game for the new console.

In the end, Sony had taken command of this attractive adjacency. The extent of its victory is truly astounding. In May 2001, at the time of Microsoft's entrance into the business, Sony sat at the top of an $18 billion global market with an installed base of more than sixty million video game players. In the United States, more than one in five households had a Sony PlayStation or its successor, PS2, with almost twenty-five million units shipped. That compared to sixteen million for its nearest rival, Nintendo's N64 machine. Sega had all but disappeared, its Saturn console garnering only 8 percent of the market.

Sony's plan to corral independent software vendors worked, as much because of the level playing field that Sony created for them as for the elegance of design of its machine and development platform. Sony also succeeded, as intended, in changing the marketing of video games. As Tony Hinchliffe, one of Sega's European managers, put it after witnessing Sony's impact on consumer marketing, "It is about lifestyle now rather than being a toy." And within three years, as predicted, Sony had used its manufacturing efficiencies to drive the price of the PlayStation from $300 down to less than $100.

When Microsoft's leaders thought about entering the fray, they first examined the state of the video game industry. Was it an attractive growth market?

One thing was certain: it was very different from the industry Sony had invaded in 1994. Seven years later, the market was four times larger and still growing at double-digit rates. Aside from the appealing financials, video gaming had taken on long-term strategic importance: the video game console had become an entrée to the living room and the bedroom. It was a device that could potentially merge the power of television and personal computing. Sony was even talking about it as a platform for someday delivering video-on-demand to the home. This was big stuff, far too important for Microsoft, the world's leading technology organization, to miss out on.

Yet, there was one highly unattractive feature—the size and power of the industry's incumbents. Back in 1994, Sony attacked a market ruled by two billion-dollar companies that counted on video gaming for their entire revenue. Now, one had practically dropped out, but the other, Nintendo, was much larger and had diversified into hand-held video gaming with its lucrative $3 billion Game Boy franchise. Sony, a huge, sophisticated, multifaceted, deep-pocketed competitor, dominated the industry. It had smoothly transitioned to a 128-bit machine, named the PS2, and another major technical evolution wasn't expected for three more years. Sony had cleverly designed the PS2 to play all the old console's games—a first for the industry— assuring consumers that their investment was protected. This design also provided a significant incentive for the fifty million owners of PlayStation to replace their machines with PS2s. Independent soft-ware developers all lined up with new games at the launch of PS2 and were also able to benefit from selling their older games on the new console. In less than six months, Sony had sold seven million copies of the new machine. By the time Microsoft was ready to launch its new game console, Sony had a formidable head start on that genera-tion of machines.

The video game market was still attractive, but its incumbents could be counted on to offer much greater resistance to a newcomer than Sony had encountered.

The next question: did Microsoft possess major advantages that would enable it to become market leader? To begin with, the corpo-ration was the world's most powerful producer of software, and software was at the heart of the video game industry. Second, video-gaming was going to go online, with gamers everywhere matching their skill and wits against other gamers, and Microsoft was an Internet powerhouse. Finally, the company had an advantage that it had used before to conquer competitors—cash, and lots of it. It was ready to commit $2 billion to this new adjacency, including $500 million just for marketing.

Armed with that impressive weaponry, Microsoft was ready to invade, but first it faced the third adjacency question: could its other operations match the standards of competition in the market? For example, Sony had brought world-class consumer entertainment marketing to what had previously been a toy category. Markets were segmented, consumers were targeted, and products were positioned with great planning and sophistication. Microsoft had substantially less experience in consumer marketing. After all, its stranglehold on the desktop software market hasn't required that it plumb the subtleties of product positioning, microsegmentation, or aspirational branding. Microsoft was an unabashed mass marketer with little experience in markets as competitive as video gaming.

Microsoft was also going to have to meet a different standard of competition in software. While Nintendo and Sega still controlled about one third of all the software revenue with their homegrown titles, more than three dozen independent organizations were producing dazzling games, costing upwards of $10 million to develop. Microsoft would have to either convince developers to design its games or match their work in-house. But developers were overwhelmingly loyal to Sony, and no one ever accused Microsoft of generating elegant software code or dazzling visuals.

The economics of the industry would pose another challenge. In taking on Sony, Microsoft would be facing a company capable of producing a 128-bit computer with powerful graphics, a DVD player, a nonstop operating system, and a couple of games for $300. That kind of efficiency was unknown in the personal-computer industry, even for Dell.

Microsoft's results with the Xbox as of the end of 2002, more than a year after the launch of its product, were disappointing, but not disastrous. With worldwide sales of eight million consoles, it was tied with Nintendo for second place. But Sony was far ahead, and Microsoft's growth had been earned with losses of more than $1.5 billion. At Sony, meanwhile, video gaming is its most profitable business.

The advantages that were supposed to yield a victory have not worked out as planned. Microsoft's software capabilities, for instance, have not translated into winning games, with the exception of the critically acclaimed Halo, which accompanied the Xbox launch. Nor did the organization succeed in attracting hot, independently produced games to its console. Japanese developers, for example, have been put off by Microsoft's very businesslike attitude toward the games. "Americans take a dry approach," says Arihiro Nakamura, chief executive and president of game developer Tecmo. "They identify how much value, they analyze numbers. Japanese business begins with, 'Do you love our business?'" To fill the software void, Microsoft has begun acquiring video game developers.

Another advantage Microsoft counted on, its Internet expertise, has been blunted by slow growth in the demand for online video gaming. To make matters worse, the Xbox was designed with online gaming in mind, so it carries more elaborate chip sets and a higher cost of manufacture than its competitors' consoles. Since Microsoft contracts out the manufacture of its machine, its ability to chop costs is limited. Meanwhile, Sony has been cutting the price of the PS2 to just above its market-leading manufacturing cost, so Microsoft loses more than $100 for every console that it sells. In a market where consoles sell in the millions that can add up to real money.

Both Microsoft and Nintendo were late to the 128-bit console party, and both have suffered at the hands of Sony as a result. "Sony had a tremendous head start," says J. Allard, general manager for the Xbox. "I'm focused on making sure there's no gap next time around." But that means hanging in until 2005, when the next shift in video gaming is expected. In the meantime, Sony is locking software developers into exclusive arrangements on 128-bit games.

As both the Sony and Microsoft cases attest, adjacent growth is a challenging business. Many companies have failed in their attempts to conquer neighboring markets. Let's take a closer look at the three key adjacency questions and some of the pitfalls of this growth discipline.

Is It a Promising Market?

Twenty-three years ago, Michael Porter translated the basics of microeconomics into a simple and coherent framework for analyzing markets. In *Competitive Advantage,* he wrote that markets were affected by five forces: rivalry among competitors, the bargaining powers of customers and of suppliers, and the threats of new entrants and of substitute products. The five-forces model remains the most effective method for analyzing the attractiveness of a stable, slow-changing market. The problem is, those are not the kind of markets to consider as a target for adjacent growth.

To begin with, they are not likely to provide double-digit growth. Beyond that, when a market is stable, and the incumbents are not distracted by the issues instability brings, they can turn all their energies to preventing you from gaining a foothold. Also, as the new arrival, you're in a hurry to find out whether your market entry was the right decision. Incumbents have a longer time horizon, so they are willing to sacrifice short-term performance for the larger goal of keeping competitors out.

That's what happened to Procter & Gamble when it tried to muscle its way into the orange-juice business. P&G launched Citrus Hill Fresh Choice in 1982, taking on Coca-Cola's Minute Maid and Beatrice's Tropicana brands. The result? Both organizations massively increased their promotional budgets to blunt the effect of Procter's

THE FOURTH DISCIPLINE · 173

$100 million advertising campaign. Coke also alerted the U.S. Food and Drug Administration about Procter, which eventually had to remove the word *Fresh* from its label. After a few years and hundreds of millions of dollars of losses, P&G gave up and left the orange-juice market to the incumbents.

So Procter learned the hard way that any assessment of industry attractiveness must include due consideration of the likely competitive response. It also learned to be wary of entering stable markets controlled by a few strong incumbents. Had the company's leaders thought, just for a moment, about how they would react to a potentially powerful new entrant in the toothpaste business, they might have saved their company a considerable headache, not to mention a considerable amount of cash.

As suggested above, the opportunity for adjacent-market growth improves when the market is in flux, when incumbents are busy adjusting to change and thus have less time to focus on new entrants and fewer weapons with which to fight.

The problem is, dynamic markets are inherently more difficult to assess accurately. Many businesses come running when a developing market begins to blossom. They want to get in on the action, but few of them are apt to succeed. That kind of scenario is developing today in the market for fuel-cell technology: everyone from Hitachi and Sanyo to Motorola and General Motors is crowding in to join Ballard Power Systems and United Technology, which have been toiling away for years to bring this technology to the mass market.

The lesson to be learned: if you're going to enter a dynamic adjacent market, you must time your entry carefully. Too early, and you throw away your resources on a market that won't ripen for years. Too late, and you have to cope with established, hostile incumbents.

One familiar form of the dynamic market that attracts new entrants seeking adjacency growth occurs because of a generational shift in technology, process, or customer value. That was what was happening in video games when Sony entered the market as it was shifting from sixteen-bit to thirty-two-bit processors. Entrenched competitors, eager to protect their base of business, usually delay embracing the new technology or process, opening an opportunity for adjacent-market entry. But generational shifts are far from guaranteed opportunities. Remember, Microsoft bet that the video game business was on the brink of moving online. Two years later it's still on the brink, an expensive lesson in bad timing.

In general, companies do a mediocre job of analyzing the attractiveness of an adjacent market because they are outsiders looking in, without the hard-earned knowledge that has become almost instinctive to incumbents. Newcomers assess the possibilities on paper, rather than on the basis of experience.

Can You Win in This Market?

Adjacent-market growth only makes sense if you have advantages over the incumbents that can gain you market leadership. Without such advantages, you are almost certainly not going to win.

Perhaps the best-known misjudgment in that regard was Mike Armstrong's decision to put together an AT&T telecom supermarket, gathering local, long-distance, wireless, Internet, and cable services under one roof. The magic word was *integration*. Cable would allow AT&T to tap directly into the home and office, giving it the entrée to sell and deliver a single, convenient bundle of offerings—and that was only the start. Armstrong envisioned a stream of innovative new services, such as interactive television and video-on-demand, which would justify his expensive acquisitions.

"You will find a huge return on investment," crowed Dan Somers, AT&T's new cable head and its former CFO, after the company had completed back-to-back acquisitions of two huge cable companies. "This is the biggest home run in American history."

But it's one thing to talk about using your advantages in a new market, and quite another to execute your plan. AT&T struggled to upgrade the acquired cable-television systems to digital. It fumbled in trying to produce unified call-center support, a single-service call, and an integrated monthly bill. In other words, the enterprise could not pull it off before other offers and other solutions flooded the market. The cost to shareholders? More than $150 billion of market value.

It wasn't that Armstrong's ideas were off base. Cable, Internet access, and local telephone services were attractive adjacent markets. AT&T actually had advantages that might have enabled it to prevail, but the public wasn't going to dance to AT&T's tune simply because the company had a plan. It required top-notch execution and follow-through, which were nowhere in sight, and, as a result, the offer went untested and unexploited. The shareholder was left to pay the price.

The lesson was clear: competitive differentiation in an adjacent market must be built on advantages that are tangible and practical, not on future plans and visionary possibilities.

Armstrong's blunder with AT&T is reminiscent of another dead-on-arrival adjacency fantasy concocted by Richard Ferris when he was CEO of Allegis. You don't remember Allegis? That would disappoint Ferris, since he spent more than $1 million in 1987 just to find the name. Allegis was Ferris's misguided bid to put together Westin Hotels, United Airlines, and Hertz car rentals as one integrated enterprise, focused on the business traveler. That might have worked if there weren't thousands of destinations where United didn't fly and Westin didn't have a hotel. What Ferris bought, while extensive, was hardly a one-stop solution for business travelers venturing beyond major U.S. cities. And if that weren't handicap enough, Allegis never got around to actually integrating the businesses to provide some unique value to the customer who purchased all three services.

In Allegis, Richard Ferris misjudged the business-travel market, underestimated what would be needed to serve it as an integrated enterprise, overrated his capabilities, and—above all—failed to meet the competitive standards of the industry. It is hard to imagine a more complete catastrophe.

In contrast to AT&T and Allegis, Sony built its advantage on capabilities that were tangible, practical, and easily implemented.

Can You Match the Standards of Competition in This Market?

Given your advantages, and assuming that they can put incumbent companies on the defensive, you must still determine whether you have the skills and resources to run with competitors. You don't have to defeat the enemy in every corner of the battlefield, but you do have to meet the quality level that is common in the market.

These standards of competition must be met in three areas: the technology that underpins the products or services the industry sells; the relationships you have with customers, distributors, suppliers, and other industry stakeholders with whom you must partner; and the business-model design you have chosen to create value for your customers, investors, and other stakeholders. Failure to measure up in any one of the three areas spells disaster.

Defense contractors never seem to be able to learn this lesson. That's why they have such difficulty growing in adjacent commercial markets. They too often assume that if they have truly advanced technology that has a real application in the market, they can easily push in and beat entrenched competitors. A classic example of this syndrome was Grumman Aircraft's decision to use its plane-building technology to produce aluminum canoes after World War II. There was nothing wrong with the technology, and the market for canoes was wide open after years of wartime shortages. But Grumman didn't understand the market and could never find the balance of price and value that would make a profit.

Financial-services organizations have also had difficulty learning this truth. They have been tempted by the illusion that, because they have powerful customer relationships, their customers will happily buy products from other markets. That was the thinking that sparked all those unsuccessful financial-supermarket models of the 1980s, when banks tried to cross-peddle investments, insurance, and other financial products to their retail customers. These efforts failed because the banks understood neither the technology nor the business models necessary for success in those other markets. Many commercial banks created abysmal investment records in mutual funds, for example, because they didn't possess the investment know-how—the technology—of Fidelity or Merrill Lynch. In payroll services, they didn't have the slick business models of Paychex or ADP. They could only offer me-too products developed by other corporations. Their customers saw no distinctive value in the offerings and stayed away in droves.

But financial supermarkets may finally have come of age. Fidelity Investments, Charles Schwab, and giants CitiGroup and Merrill Lynch are all making headway in offering one-stop shopping in investments, brokerage services, banking, and mortgages because they have bought or built first-class capabilities in each of the markets in which they compete. More important, the new financial supermarkets are beginning to come up with offerings that create real value for their clients across the board—meeting the standards of competition.

One of the grand illusions of adjacency growth is that "because I have a sophisticated business model, I can automatically apply it to an adjacent market and rout the incumbents." Amazon.com made that assumption when it announced that it was applying its bookselling model to all retail markets. The move failed, predictably, because retail markets have many varied characteristics, and a business model that works in one almost surely can't be applied to all of them. Without the specific know-how concerning promotions, merchandise management, and logistics, and without key supplier and channel relationships, Amazon has had a tough time outside of books and music, Amazon's traditional markets. It has taken mountains of losses to convince Jeff Bezos, Amazon's founder, that his company cannot simply waltz into adjacent retail markets and take them over.

You must have 80 percent of the capabilities you need to match your competitors' standards in technology, market relationships, and business model design to hold your own. Of course, you also need to have major advantages over your rivals that will tip the market in your direction.

Make Versus Buy

As so often in seeking to achieve double-digit growth, you face two choices as to the approach you use to invade an adjacent market: you can try to use your current skills and resources to carve out a place, or you can buy your way into the market.

Each choice has its strengths and weaknesses. An organic approach that relies on your existing advantages seems like the easier way to unseat your rivals, but it also means that the organization has to learn how to meet every standard of competition in the marketplace. You are all too likely to miss important market nuances, underestimate the importance of certain market relationships, or understand too late that your company does not possess all the requisite technology capabilities.

Acquiring a company or companies to build up the needed resources and skills does make it easier to meet the standards of competition, since you now possess a functioning entity in the market. (Buying a business that is failing will obviously not fulfill that requirement, though companies do it all the time.) A decent acquisition obviously kick-starts your entry into the market, at least initially.

But to realize a lasting advantage from an acquisition, you need to achieve a substantial degree of integration with the parent company.

You will recall that in acquiring businesses for market share gain, your best approach is to dismember and digest the acquired organization. Adjacent acquisitions, on the other hand, must remain as separate enterprises, with capabilities and business models distinct from those of the acquirer's, but integration for management control and for transfer of capability advantages is essential. While management control integration can be mandated through systems and technology, knowledge transfer in technology, market relationships, or business model design is more delicate work. It is usually best accomplished by first transferring management talent between the two businesses.

Rockwell Collins provides an example of the challenges of integrating an adjacent-market acquisition. The corporation began as Collins Radio in 1933, producing shortwave radio equipment; it gained a measure of international fame by making it possible for Admiral Richard Byrd's crew to communicate with the world on its expedition to the South Pole. Today, the company's core markets are in defense electronics and avionics, the cockpit instrumentation in commercial aircraft. Under Clay Jones's leadership, Rockwell Collins has also made the most of its technology skills and deep relationships with Boeing, Airbus, and commercial airlines to successfully enter a number of adjacent markets, including in-flight entertainment systems.

The company's entry into this market adjacency came in December 1997, when it acquired Hughes-Avicom International, a leading producer of in-flight entertainment equipment. Hughes had a new total entertainment system in its pipeline, and when it rolled out the following year, the Rockwell Collins sales force helped to ensure that it was a major success. The system is now standard in first class on most international flights.

The company has built a $400 million business in this adjacency since then, despite the adverse conditions of the airline industry and despite an initial standoff with Hughes-Avicom managers. The Hughes people resisted integration. They had succeeded in building the business at Hughes by remaining independent of the satellite businesses that had few capabilities that were of advantage in in-flight entertainment. This resistance to integration continued under Rockwell Collins's ownership, despite the ample advantages in technology and aviation relationships that the parent company could bring. Rockwell Collins managers, in turn, treated the new acquisition gingerly, not wanting to stifle originality or trigger defections. In hindsight, Rockwell Collins believes it would have made faster progress if it had folded the new team into closer alignment from the start.

The point to remember: acquisitions can give you a head start in an adjacent market, especially when it comes to meeting the standards of competition, but they require a lot more work to establish synergies that will create a competitive advantage.

Healthy Adjacent Growth

For an example of a company that has entered adjacent markets with great success, using both the make and buy approaches, consider Johnson & Johnson. The company has chalked up sixty-nine consecutive years of sales increases, including a rise from $22.6 billion to $36.3 billion in revenues from 1997 to 2002, a compound annual growth rate of 10 percent, and eighteen straight years of double-digit earnings increases.

Johnson & Johnson dates its origin to 1876, when founder Robert Wood Johnson first attended a talk by Sir Joseph Lister. Lister had discovered that germs—"invisible assassins," he called them—were responsible for a post-operative mortality rate that exceeded 90 percent in some hospitals. Johnson and two of his brothers began producing sterile surgical dressings in 1886 and eventually won over a very skeptical medical profession.

Dressings led to sterilized catgut sutures and then to adhesive plaster, still primarily for the hospital market. It was in 1921 that the company invaded its first adjacent market, home healthcare, with the marketing of Johnson's Baby Cream and what is still its most famous and widely used product, the Band-Aid. Through the next few decades, J&J moved into adjacencies mainly by internal expansion, first creating a product and then splitting off a division to market a whole product line. Thus, a sanitary napkin led to the Modess division, which became today's Personal Products subsidiary. A single birth-control product became the Ortho division and then Ortho Pharmaceutical. An Ethicon division, specializing in sutures, has spawned two separate surgical-product subsidiaries.

In recent years, while the company still moves into some adjacencies with internal efforts, it more often uses alliances and acquisitions to invade adjacent markets, and it has no hesitation in leaving those that no longer fit into its long-term strategy. Between 1989 and 1999, for example, J&J made forty-five acquisitions of companies or product lines and sold off eighteen businesses. It concentrates on three broad market sectors: pharmaceutical products, medical devices and diagnostics, and consumer healthcare. Its management is structured to encourage continued learning and the leveraging of its skills and knowledge across its many units.

J&J's adjacency skills begin with market assessment. Because of its long familiarity with the science and technology of healthcare and its thorough understanding of both the professional and the consumer sides of the field, the company's managers consistently find profitable and growing new markets nearby. Aside from those winning advantages it brings to any adjacency, the corporation also maintains an international marketing and distribution advantage through its in-depth relationships with a huge network of doctors, hospitals, drugstores, and mass retailers.

Typically, J&J spots an adjacent market that it sees as having huge potential growth and moves into it with a fairly modest acquisition. Thus, in 1986, it bought LifeScan, a small producer of blood glucose meters and test strips for diabetics. The new subsidiary had sales of only $22.8 million, and it cost J&J just $81 million. But J&J's reading of the market potential was dead-on. Worldwide, there are now at least one hundred million diabetes patients, and LifeScan's revenues in 1999 totaled $1 billion. The world market for self-testing, whole-blood glucose products came to $3.5 billion in 2000 and is expected to double by 2010.

But that modest acquisition led to a much bigger one in 2002. One of LifeScan's suppliers was Inverness Medical, a producer and developer of advanced blood glucose monitors. Most of its $100 million in revenues actually came from LifeScan, which was marketing its technology under license. One Inverness system, for example, lets patients test themselves in just five seconds, using a minuscule sampling of blood, which is taken from the forearm—a much less painful experience than the traditional finger-stick. J&J saw so much potential in Inverness that it paid $1.2 billion to get control of its technology and consolidate its market position.

Occasionally, J&J moves into an adjacent market with an immediate major acquisition, as it did in skin care in 1994 with the purchase of Neutrogena. At the time, Neutrogena was known mainly for its mild, clear soap; it had revenues of more than $300 million, and the purchase cost J&J $924 million. But J&J broadened the Neutrogena brand through internal expansion, branching into men's products, cosmetics, and such specialized products as acne treatment. In that new line, Neutrogena rapidly grew to take over 25 percent of the entire U.S. market.

J&J used four of its core strengths to make the Neutrogena purchase work. Its long-standing relationship with dermatologists bolstered Neutrogena's hypoallergenic products; its research-and-development skills led to a tenfold increase in the total product line; J&J's consumer marketing and advertising expanded awareness and broadened the appeal of the Neutrogena brand; and J&J's distribution clout got Neutrogena into supermarkets and big-box stores and improved its positioning on drugstore shelves.

Having sized up skin care as a desirable adjacent growth opportunity, Johnson & Johnson decided that it possessed the advantages, cited above, to take on the market's incumbents. To leverage those advantages, and ensure at least a temporary ability to meet competitive standards in the market, J&J bought Neutrogena as a platform for future adjacent growth.

One essential factor in making the acquisition a long-term success, though, was the ability of J&J's managers to meld Neutrogena into their decentralized operating structure without disrupting its success. Jeff Nugent, a veteran J&J executive, was placed in charge of the new business as soon as it was acquired. Nugent understood how to leverage J&J's vast capabilities through technology councils, joint projects with sibling divisions, and consultations with experienced executives from other parts of the parent organization.

When your own market is going through a dry patch, when no segments seem to offer the double-digit growth you deserve, adjacent markets seem like a natural and relatively easy substitute target. After all, you know a lot about the business already, and you have a shrewd idea of what you have to do to learn the rest. But as this chapter has noted, there are potential pitfalls on every side. And sometimes, because of economic conditions or the overwhelming power of incumbents, the adjacencies are simply unattractive.

When those circumstances prevail, another alternative exists: leave the neighborhood altogether, and jump into a whole new line of business. Of course, it's a dangerous path, where most of the advantages an organization enjoys within its industry, and within an adjacency, are of little or no value. It means that managers must approach that option with all the care and risk management exercised by an oil exploration team embarked on a new-field wildcat.

How to think about invading an unfamiliar business, and how to proceed once a go decision has been made, are the subject of the next chapter. One hint of what's to come: managers must learn to think more like investors.

8

The Fifth Discipline:

Invest in New Lines of Business

As 2002 ended, Gerry Schwartz sat in his office overlooking the shoreline of Lake Ontario and reflected on his company's progress. He had founded Onex Corporation in 1984 with Cdn$50 million and enormous ambition. By 1995, it was a US$4.3 billion organization with thriving businesses in auto parts, airline catering, and food distribution. Not bad for ten years, but nothing compared to Onex's track record since. By 2003, it had become one of the five largest companies in Canada, with revenues of $14.4 billion, adding sugar refining, electronics manufacturing, and movie theaters to Onex's business portfolio. What is Schwartz's secret? Just this: he and his team have mastered the discipline of entering totally new and disparate markets as a means of achieving double-digit growth.

Wait just one minute, I hear you saying. Isn't Onex's willy-nilly invasion of disconnected markets reminiscent of the "conglomeration" fad of the late 1960s when executives such as Harold Geneen, Charles Bluhdorn, and Ben Heinemann pasted together vast, pastiche empires that eventually fell of their own weight and left shareholders gnashing their teeth? Haven't we been assured by our betters that unrelated diversification is a loser's strategy?

We have, and, generally speaking, it is. But as this chapter will demonstrate, if you know what you're doing, and your company has the human and financial resources to execute your ideas, major growth through new lines of business may be appropriate for you. This fifth discipline of growth is a high-wire act, yet it could just fit your needs—especially if the other four disciplines can't deliver all the growth that your firm desires.

What makes it risky is the fact that your company is not likely to have any core advantages in these distant markets, much less any capacity to match the standards of competition. Incumbents hold all the cards. That's why any effort to build your own business in unrelated markets is virtually doomed. That's why your best bet is to buy your way in. And that explains why winning in distant markets is not so much a management challenge as it is an investment challenge. It requires a special mind-set.

Gerry Schwartz has it. He started down the investing track in the private-equity department at Bear Stearns, whose alumni include such leveraged buyout luminaries as Henry Kravis, George Roberts, and Ted Forstmann. At Onex, his formidable investment expertise has worked miracles—spotting far-afield opportunities, putting together advantageous deals, keeping a check-rein on the acquired organizations.

In 1996, Schwartz put Onex into electronics manufacturing services just as that market was taking off. Large electronics companies, such as Nokia and Cisco, had begun outsourcing their manufacturing capacity to highly efficient independent companies. Onex negotiated the purchase of some of IBM's in-house manufacturing capacity, which included about $2 billion worth of business under contract. The acquisition cost $560 million, but it placed Onex in a market that was predicted to grow 25 percent per year. In rapid-fire succession, Onex added additional capacity and new contracts from Hewlett-Packard, Lucent, and more than thirty other electronics companies. By 2002, Schwartz had built the business, now named Celestica, into an $8.3 billion global competitor. Along the way, he sold shares in the business to the public, though retaining voting control.

What experience did Onex have in electronics manufacturing services before 1996? None. What synergies did its other businesses bring to this acquisition? None.

In 1997, it was the sugar-refining market that caught Schwartz's attention. He acquired BC Sugar Refinery, a public company, in a transaction valued at $395 million. Immediately the company was reorganized and some assets, including a marginally profitable U.S. refining division, were sold, returning the full purchase price to Onex, which then set to work helping management cut operating and overhead costs at the refinery. The result is that Onex now owns a sweet business that cost it nothing and produces $180 million in revenues and $35 million in operating earnings.

In April 1998, Onex jumped into call-center management with the purchase of a 250-person company. Six months later, Schwartz made another acquisition in this market, an organization with two thousand employees and annual revenues of $125 million. Three months after that, a third business was added to the fold. As of 2003, the call-center unit was generating more than $400 million in sales. Again, Onex had no prior experience or advantage in the market.

One more way-out Onex move: in 1999, it made a small investment in a startup called Galaxy Entertainment, which focused on operating multiplex movie theaters in midsized Canadian cities. In 2002, Onex really upped the ante by acquiring Loews Cineplex, Star Theatres, and Cinemex in Mexico. As of a year later, the movie-theater businesses were delivering $950 million of profitable annual revenue for Onex.

Onex's financial performance through this period has been spectacular. Over the past five years, a share of Onex stock has outperformed GE, Microsoft, Berkshire Hathaway, and almost all of the other companies on *Fortune*'s list of most-admired companies. Revenues since the end of 1995 have grown at a compound annual rate of 19 percent. Since the organization was founded in 1984, annual return on invested capital has averaged 29 percent.

At its core, Onex is a leveraged buyout firm, along the lines of KKR and Forstmann Little—but with a difference. For one, its stock is publicly traded. For another, it is in no rush to cash in. The company buys businesses with an eye toward operating them for the long term, unconstrained by the hold periods of typical private equity funds. As Onex's corporate statement of principles puts it, "If a company is good enough to buy, it is good enough to be vigorously developed for the long term."

Investors Versus Managers

The high-powered investment skills to be found in Onex's small staff stand in contrast to the management skills that dominate the upper ranks of most large companies.

Good managers have a passion for the marketplace and for their business—they are deeply committed and have a broad understanding of what makes their operation work. Good managers thrive on challenges and maintain an optimistic, can-do approach to problems. They have the fire to lead the troops through the worst as well as the best of times.

Good investors, on the other hand, keep their passion for the bedroom. They are, by definition, objective, refusing to allow emotion to affect their judgment as to the virtues and shortcomings of a company and a market opportunity. Good investors are generally not inclined or equipped to lead the troops, whom they must view with an unsentimental eye. They are realists, not optimists, maybe even a touch cynical; if they err, it is on the side of conservatism. They are also patient. They pass up one hundred opportunities for every one taken.

Here are some other mandates of the successful acquisitions investor:

• Never overpay for a new line of business. When the price gets too high, good investors walk away from a potential acquisition, no matter how prized the prey, how perfect the strategic fit, or how exciting the market. That's why Onex lost Labatt's, Canada's second-largest brewer, to a Belgian acquirer. Though Schwartz had worked on the deal for a long time and his team had convinced itself that it wanted to own this business, in the end economics, not emotion, decided the issue. That ability to walk away helps explain why virtually all of the company's new lines of business look like bargains verging on outright steals. One dramatic example: Onex invested only about $195 million of its own capital in the electronics manufacturing business starting in 1996, but by the end of 2002 its stake was worth more than $979 million.

• Find simple strategies. The people at Onex know from experience that the more complex the strategy, the less likely it will ever come to pass. Instead, they look for businesses and markets where value can be unlocked through steady, practical operational improvements. For instance, Onex originally purchased Sky Chefs, the airline catering company, for just over $23 million in capital. It saw the need for airline caterers to operate across wider geographies and grow in efficiency to meet the needs of global airline alliances. It started by buying an organization that operated in one country with American Airlines as its only large client, and then expanded the business organically and through acquisitions to become the world's largest airline caterer, serving more than 230 airlines on five continents. Steady progress in globalization and efficiency was the basis of a winning value creation strategy. Onex took out cash over sixteen years of ownership, and, in a brilliant display of timing, sold the remaining 47 percent to Lufthansa for more than $840 million in 2001, just before the most severe downturn the airline industry has ever seen. For Onex, Sky Chefs produced compound annual returns of 31 percent over a sixteen-year period. Not bad.

• Partner with your new line of business. The investor discipline requires that you invest as much in the management you acquire as in a market, a business, or a plan. Onex subsidiaries operate independently, with each chief executive given considerable autonomy, but Schwartz and his small headquarters staff pay close attention to the details. "Acquisitions are made in partnership with the purchased company's management," the corporate principles declare. "We operate their business together—as partners." And since successful businesses are built by successful leaders, the assessment of the leadership team is as important to a decision to buy into a new line of business as is the target's balance sheet.

The successes of corporations such as Onex have a lot to teach us, but I suspect we learn more from other companies' mistakes. Let's look at a couple of examples.

A Bitter Brew for Starbucks

In so many ways, the Starbucks chain of coffee shops is a poster boy for outstanding growth delivered by a smart, sophisticated management team. Since the end of 1997, the company has increased revenues, gross profits, and net income an average of 25.9, 27.3, and 33.2 percent per year, respectively. Those are frothy numbers. Buried within that performance, though, were some missteps into new lines of business that cost the corporation its unbroken string of profit rises and temporarily distracted management from its core growth opportunities.

In the mid-1990s, when the brand first showed its power, Starbucks had two core businesses—its cafes and the sale of whole-bean coffee, both through its own outlets and through select retail groceries. Soon, though, management was besieged with propositions for new ventures coming from every imaginable quarter.

The company moved cautiously and chalked up some successes—notably in adjacent-market opportunities, where it partnered with Pepsi in bottled drinks and with Dryers in coffee-flavored ice cream. In both cases, Starbucks contributed its core advantages—its powerful brand and its expertise in coffee flavor formulation—while its partners met the standards of competition with their manufacturing, distribution, and marketing expertise.

After these successes and a few small disappointments, Starbucks systematically studied its various options in adjacent markets and came to three smart conclusions: First, if an opportunity didn't bolster the core brand's power, then the deal wasn't worth doing. Second, a deal had to be highly financially attractive. Third, the company recognized the limits of its core capabilities and decided that going it alone in adjacent markets was not the preferred option.

Then along came the Internet frenzy, and Starbucks, like so many other companies, lost its cool. Perhaps it was the proximity of high-tech Seattle neighbors such as Amazon.com and Microsoft, beckoning irresistibly from the Web. However hip Starbucks was, its business was fundamentally old-economy. Now, however, it defined itself as a "lifestyle" enterprise and plunged into a series of minority investments in Internet sites that supported and extended the sophisticated, urbane lifestyle to which its customers aspired. Starbucks invested in sites for chat, cooking accessories, and home delivery. What any of them had to do with Starbucks's core competencies was never clear, and, in 2000, the company wrote off nearly everything it had put up—$60 million. That was about six months' worth of earnings for the whole organization.

The surrender was prompt and timely. It stanched the bloodletting, but the company's profit for that year dipped below the 1999 level, even though the core businesses continued to grow and prosper.

Starbucks's experience is a prime example of an altogether too familiar phenomenon—a company caught in the no-man's-land between an adjacency and a new line of business. It happens this way: Your company has certain advantages in your own market that you believe will yield success in what you take to be an adjacent market, and you assume that your considerable operating capabilities will enable you to meet the standards of competition. You make your move—and suddenly discover that the market is actually not a neighbor but a distant stranger. Your advantages are irrelevant; your capabilities are insufficient; you are mired in no-man's-land.

It all starts with fuzzy thinking about what creates competitive advantage. In the case of Starbucks, it was that fuzzy lifestyle concept that blurred management's strategic vision and prevented the corporation from approaching the new market with the detached cynicism of an investor.

A Bad Time for Swatch

Hear the name Swatch, and you automatically summon up an image of the brightly colored, inexpensive wristwatch that swept the lower end of the watch market two decades ago. But there is a lot more to know about the Swatch Group, which is headquartered in Biel, Switzerland. The company has done a marvelous job of positioning itself in every segment of the watch market, top to bottom, by buying up a host of brands including Omega, Tissot, Blancpain, Rado, Longines, Certina, Mido, Balmain, and Hamilton. In fact, it is the world's largest manufacturer and distributor of finished watches, with 160 production centers, most of them in Switzerland, but others in the United States, France, Germany, Italy, the Virgin Islands, Thailand, Malaysia, and China.

Swatch has also grown by invading adjacent markets. It supplies the entire Swiss watch industry with movements. It has leveraged its expertise in tiny electronic watch mechanisms to become a supplier of microelectronics and micromechanics to the computer, telecommunications, medical applications, automotive, and electronics industries. The Swatch Group is also active in the service sector, and provides timing for the Olympic Games and other international sports events.

In 1988, the corporation began producing telephone handsets, first in the United States, then in Europe. The theory was that the combination of Swatch's microelectronics know-how and brand appeal made the handset market an adjacency where those advantages would enable Swatch to conquer. But by 1988, corded telephones were already a commodity, and Swatch's technology could provide very little advantage. The company spruced up the colors, added a twin-line feature and cordless models, but never captured more than a few percent of this low-margin market. The basic problem: telephone handsets were not an adjacency for Swatch, they were an unrelated market, and Swatch's capabilities were nowhere near meeting the standards of competition set by Sony, Panasonic, and other leaders.

Six years later, Swatch developed an audacious plan for a new kind of automobile. Nicholas Hayak, the chief executive, who was credited with saving the Swiss watch industry from the Japanese onslaught, had in mind a vehicle that would be small, economical to drive, and ecologically friendly, with an electric or hybrid engine of Swatch's own design. It would have detachable body panels to allow customers to change colors on a whim, just as they could change their Swatch watches. The car would not be purchased but subscribed to, with monthly payments continuing indefinitely and a new car periodically substituted. Production would be highly automated, streamlined, and outsourced, a model that had worked so well for Hayak in the watch industry. The vehicle would, he thought, epitomize the new lifestyle that was emerging around the world, providing efficient and responsible mobility for the masses.

To Hayak, the automobile business looked like an adjacent market waiting to be shaken up. He thought that he could bring the corporation's core advantages in styling, electronics, and production to bear, and win big. But Hayak also knew that the auto business was complex, and there was much that his organization didn't know. To bolster its chances, Swatch soon teamed up in a fifty/fifty joint venture with Daimler Benz, a prestigious carmaker, but one that had no experience producing small, economical automobiles.

The joint venture barely survived the launch of the first vehicle. Originally slated to debut in April 1998, it had to be pushed back because the test models kept tipping over in a standard stability test. Swatch's electric and hybrid engine designs never got off the drawing board, so the first cars had traditional gasoline and diesel motors. When the vehicles finally appeared that fall, public curiosity did not translate into substantial sales. The joint venture had expected to sell two hundred thousand automobiles that first year, but managed just eighty thousand.

Here is what one reviewer had to say about the car on its debut at the Paris Auto Show: "There are three drawbacks to the scheme. The non-gear auto transmission doesn't work as well as hoped, the car actually costs about 60,000 francs, which is a lot for a little, and, if you don't like Swatch watches, it is possible you won't like this car much either. Mercedes is said to be waiting for first registration statistics with some anxiety."

Daimler Benz's anxiety turned to disgust. Like the pig and the chicken at a ham-and-egg breakfast, one party was committed, but the other was merely involved. Daimler Benz terminated Swatch's involvement by buying it out of the joint venture in November 1998. It also got rid of the management team and installed Andreas Renschler as president. He was a rising star at Daimler. He has scaled back expectations for the Swatch car and now hopes to turn a profit by 2005. That is after eleven years of effort and $3 billion of losses.

The next new market that Swatch tackled was the Internet. In 1998, eager to get in on the party, Swatch developed a new standard for timekeeping—Internet Time—based on dividing the day into one thousand "beats." Ground zero for Internet Time would be Swatch headquarters in Biel. Reportedly, the people in Greenwich, England, were not amused—nor was the world willing to make every timepiece obsolete by switching to a decimal time system.

That same year, Swatch looked to the mobile-phone market as a place for growth. The company was already a small producer of corded and cordless handsets, and it supplied Nokia, Motorola, and other manufacturers with quartz crystals for their phones. This time Swatch planned to take a page from Dick Tracy and produce a wrist phone, pushing its watchmaking advantage into another market. A prototype was produced, but it was bulky and had poor phone characteristics. Ultimately, Swatch determined that consumers didn't really want to wear their phones on their wrists, and the product was never launched. Undeterred, the company began work on a Web watch that would allow consumers to surf the Web from their wrists. That, too, was scrapped because of "technical questions."

There is a pattern to all this madness: Swatch kept wandering into markets where it possessed a theoretical advantage, but not the practical core capabilities for pulling it off. Again and again, the corporation found itself caught between the allure of a perceived advantage and the reality of difficult standards of competition. Inevitably, the organization has beaten a hasty retreat in almost every new market it has entered.

What Went Wrong at Starbucks and Swatch

If the managers at Starbucks and Swatch had been thinking like investors, they would have been a lot more skeptical about their new ventures. A cold-eyed look at the Internet would have shown Starbucks that it knew nothing about bits and bytes, let alone selling pots and pans or making home deliveries. A hard-nosed sniff at the auto market would have told Swatch that it had no business there, no matter how potent its styling and its brand and how much expertise Daimler Benz brought to the match.

Swatch also took the highly risky path of trying to enter new lines of business organically. Most companies that succeed in new lines of business rely on acquisitions. The odds of success in a new market where you have limited advantages are heavily stacked against you, so it's better to buy a business that has the specialized knowledge and skills you will need to compete and win.

But, even then, caution is the watchword. Note how Onex Corporation entered most of its new markets—with a small acquisition. Once it has gained comfort with the business and the management team, it is now ready to grow the business larger, but from a position inside the industry. This way, a small acquisition can convert a high-risk new line of business move into a more manageable challenge.

Buy Your Way to New Growth

Companies that successfully grow in new lines of business have three characteristics in common. They know how to identify, evaluate, and select new lines of business and potential acquisitions; value and structure acquisition deals; and exert financial, managerial, and strategic control over the acquired businesses.

Let's look at each of these in turn.

Find the Right Market and Acquisition Target. Good investors focus first on the big things, those aspects that are most crucial to success and are most difficult to change once you have committed. That means you should start by deciding what marketplace to enter. Naturally, you want a market in which participants are likely to prosper. A growing, high-margin industry covers a lot of management mistakes. Ask anyone in pharmaceuticals.

Once a marketplace is chosen, you need to answer three critical questions about any company acquisition you consider: Is it well positioned in the market? Does it have a management team that can overcome competitors and market obstacles? Does it have the right plan for success?

As suggested above, the order in which these questions are answered is important—the circumstances they deal with range from the most permanent and most difficult to correct, to the most transient and easiest to change.

To identify a good investment, you need to examine lots and lots of possibilities. In the language of a private equity investor, you need "ample deal flow." Typically, these people look at more than one hundred possibilities for every one they choose. Since most growth-obsessed companies look at far fewer potential choices, they are less likely to even get to evaluate the very best opportunities.

The first determination you make of any acquisition candidate is its positioning in your chosen market. Some market segments generate better margins, higher growth rates, and more stability than others, and that positioning translates into financial performance in general and cash flow in particular. The current cash flow of a business largely determines the cost to acquire the business. Rare is the management team that can put up impressive numbers in a disadvantaged part of even an attractive market.

I have ranked a company's management team above its strategic plans for one simple reason: a great team with a flawed plan will always defeat the best of plans in the hands of an average management team. After all, a great plan is only valid until market conditions change and that happens with alarming frequency; a great management team can be great indefinitely, constantly adjusting to changing circumstances.

The right plan is going to be simple, practical, and eminently achievable. Remember Onex's plan in its move into airline catering? Improve efficiency and operate as one company across a wider area. Its CEO directed the management team in pursuit of that simple, practical strategy for sixteen years, and it paid off enormously. Complex plans to "transform markets" or create "breakthrough customer value" should be reserved for core or adjacent markets that you know a great deal about. In new lines of business, such large plans lead to expensive lessons concerning what you failed to understand about the target, unrelated market.

Strike a Good Deal. Paying an unwarranted premium for a company is a recipe for failure in new lines of business. Yet, it is the norm in too many companies where growth in unrelated markets is driven by managerial aspirations rather than investment judgment.

How does Warren Buffett decide how much to pay for an acquisition? Like all great investors, he is dispassionate. A takeover premium may make sense, he has said, but only if the buyer's stock is overvalued or the two enterprises will earn more combined than they would separately. Since few acquirers want to concede they are overvalued, most of them predict major synergies. Usually, those advantages are an illusion, especially among buyers who pump out their company's shares for acquisitions in a kind of chain-letter scheme. When CEOs become fixated on a foolish acquisition, you can be sure their staff and outside advisors will come up with supporting projections. As Buffett puts it, "Only in fairy tales are emperors told that they are naked."

Every acquisition target's valuation contains a premium above current performance even before the bidding begins. That is because value is based on expectations of future improvements in performance. To then pay a further premium on top of this is to bet that you can improve performance of the acquired organization beyond current expectations. To make this bet in a market that is new to your company and to which it brings little advantage requires a certain amount of hubris.

Deal structuring is an art form that the wily investor uses to limit risk and encourage management. Wherever possible, they use "earnouts," which make their purchase price contingent on future performance, and instruments such as convertible debt and preferred shares, which place them first in line to get their money back if things go wrong. These same techniques are available to traditional corporate acquirers, but they add balance-sheet complexity that most big-company CFOs don't like. The result is that most traditional corporations shoulder more risk than they have to in many of their acquisitions outside their core markets.

Keep Control. When you acquire a company in a new line of business, you should not integrate its operations into your own, but rather maintain it as an independent base for growth. What does need to be integrated into the parent corporation is the newcomer's management team.

Schwartz and Buffett use remarkably similar techniques in exerting managerial control over their lines of business. They focus principally on choosing businesses with superior leadership and providing them with the correct incentives.

"Our all-stars have exactly the jobs they want, ones that they hope and expect to keep throughout their business lifetimes," Buffett writes in one of his fabled letters to shareholders. "They therefore concentrate solely on maximizing the long-term value of the businesses that they 'own' and love. If the businesses succeed, they have succeeded."

As we have seen, most efforts to diversify into unrelated businesses are unsuccessful, and most managers are poor investors outside their core markets. The perils of such diversification moves are many. While they go on, for example, the management teams of successful companies tend to neglect their thriving base, attempting to buy and operate other businesses that are nowhere near as profitable. There was a time, for example, when Coca-Cola's senior management was more focused on running theme parks, growing shrimp, and producing wine than on the soft drinks business. Credit Roberto Goizueta, who took over as CEO in 1981, with cleaning house and getting Coke refocused on its core businesses.

Given the pitfalls, why do companies persist in seeking growth in new lines of business?

In some cases, it is an accident. As we have seen, it is all too easy to misjudge a market as a tempting adjacency, only to find out too late that your organization is in foreign territory. Unfortunately, that reality can be hard to recognize, even long after the mistake has been made. A company often struggles for years to achieve the synergies it originally thought existed between its core business and the acquisition, blaming managerial incompetence, organization intransigence, or just plain bad luck, rather than recognizing that the advantage they thought they could bring to the acquisition was not relevant because of the vastly different terrain.

Another reason why many companies enter unfamiliar markets is the sheer imperative of growth for its own sake. Most organizations measure themselves according to their size. Their self-image, their prestige, and—perhaps crucially—the compensation of their leaders depend more on how big they are than on any other yardstick. As Warren Buffett has observed, the chief executive of the typical *For-*

tune 500 company knows its precise place on that list in terms of sales, but could not guess its ranking in the profit category. Thus, to some managers, growth opportunity, only loosely connected to the core business, becomes irresistible.

The great management thinker, Peter Drucker, offered another reason why bad deals get done. "I will tell you a secret," he said. "Deal making beats working. Deal making is exciting and fun, and working is grubby. Running anything is primarily an enormous amount of grubby detail work . . . deal making is romantic, sexy. That's why you have deals that make no sense."

So don't get carried away. Be skeptical about that apparent adjacency, and when a sexy deal beckons, take a cold shower. Above all, learn to take off your manager's rose-colored glasses and peer through the clear lens of an investor whenever you see anything even remotely like a new market. And when you spot an opportunity that meets the criteria set forth in this chapter, take a deep breath, and try it on for size. Just remember that, though the odds are against you, a new line of business can pay off. Warren Buffett and Gerry Schwartz are living testimony that it can be done.

In the final chapter just ahead, I rehearse the arguments of this book as a whole, with particular emphasis on the growth portfolio concept and its parallels with more traditional financial portfolios. There are good and bad ways of coping with growth risks as there are with investment risks. Alfred Lord Tennyson had it right: "This truth within thy mind rehearse, that in a boundless universe is boundless better, boundless worse."

9

Manage Your Portfolio
for Double-Digit Growth

For the past eight chapters, we've examined business growth and its five disciplines in microscopic detail. In this final chapter, I invite you to take a broader view, as if surveying the growth landscape through a panoramic lens.

Once again, I urge you to look upon the five disciplines as a whole—not as five separate strategies but as a portfolio of related options, much like your investment portfolio. Both portfolios require undivided attention, ensuring less risk and more growth. Both yield the best results when managed with a formal system of checks and balances, of automatic hedging rather than instinctive hunches.

Each of the five disciplines contains a wide variety of tactics and initiatives for creating growth, but uncertainty attends them all. Misjudged markets, aggressive competitors, poor execution—all these, plus sheer bad luck, can derail the best plans for any growth initiative, whether it's a seemingly smart way to retain customers or a supposedly surefire bet on a new acquisition. Positive thinking is the opium of the managers, as Marx might have put it, but assumptions backfire. In business, as in life, the certainty of uncertainty warns us to prepare simultaneously for the best and the worst. In short, spread your bets.

If you bet the future on only one or two growth initiatives, a misstep can prove fatal. That is what happened at both Corning and

Gateway, which badly overestimated demand and had no fallbacks. It is what happened at Caterpillar, which misjudged the competitive response from John Deere and Case IH, two farm equipment competitors that weren't about to roll over and make room for the Big Cat.

To cope with the risks inherent in every growth initiative, you must first identify and understand them. Then construct a growth portfolio aimed at reaching the overall objective while reducing the dangers inherent in individual growth initiatives.

Assess Growth Risk

Before launching any growth initiative, you need to consider four different types of growth risk: the first two derive from uncertainty about the marketplace; the second two are all about the risks of executing an initiative effectively.

Demand Risk. Unexpected changes in customer demand can unravel the best-laid plans, but even in stable times, there's a constant risk in customers' ever-rising expectations. We all want more for our money. We all snap at better choice, quality, and prices. Competitors turn on the heat with value innovations, and the risks increase as you move from the cozy confines of a core market to new segments, adjacent markets, and beyond.

Some markets have higher demand risk than others and competitors must work extra hard just to satisfy the customers they already have. The fashion industry is notoriously vulnerable to fickle fads and vanishing vogues; movie studios go hot and cold almost overnight as they try to divine the vagaries of popular taste. In other industries, demand risk is almost nonexistent. Banana demand, for example, can be forecast with remarkable accuracy.

Competitor Risk. As discussed in the chapter on adjacent-market growth, you can't enter a new market without risking the wrath of some incumbent who may well react like a stepped-on rattlesnake. Think of how bitterly local telephone companies have fought AT&T's entry into local service. But competitor risk is not limited to adjacent markets where interlopers are discouraged from entry. For more than two decades, domestic airlines have bloodied each other with irrational tactics such as selling seats below cost, thus plunging all competitors into common penury. This is the equivalent of setting up an industrial trust designed to achieve collective suicide. Indeed, panicky competitors on a rampage can wreck a market much faster than any aberrant change in customer buying behavior.

Galloping technological change is a frequent cause of such behavior. When all members of an industry, such as computer makers, believe they can own the market if only they monopolize the next drop-dead innovation, it makes for lethal competition and big risk for a newcomer.

Implementation Risk. Assume that a company has accurately identified demand and anticipated competitors' moves. Things can still go woefully wrong in translating plans into actions. In fact, implementation risk may be the largest risk of all.

Many companies have spent a bundle on customer relationship management (CRM) systems, believing they can markedly boost customer retention and market share. Only a minority of companies have made these systems work as advertised; most have reported mixed or negative results. The difference between the two groups is implementation risk. Note well that the success stories are built on narrow, surgically precise initiatives to improve information availability exactly where it can have the most impact on growth. Grandiose efforts to create enterprisewide customer contact and response have more or less failed.

Some growth initiatives have higher implementation risks than others. For example, Mike Armstrong's plan to create a one-stop, integrated communications company out of AT&T and its many acquisitions represented a substantial implementation risk, and it never really got off the drawing board. The implementation task was simply beyond the management team's capacity. Indeed, many a consulting firm has grown fat trying to beef up the implementation-management skills of a company whose reach has exceeded its grasp.

Operating Risk. Even after putting your growth plan into action, you're still not out of the woods. There is always the risk that breakdowns in your company's operations will undercut your competitiveness in your new market. Logistics failures lead to product shortages. Manufacturing problems compromise product quality. Service snafus send customers to the competition.

Operating risks rise with higher performance expectations and the increased complexity of delivering your product. FedEx, for example, manages higher operating risks than J. B. Hunt Transport because it delivers packages against tougher service commitments, requiring a more complex operating model.

Every growth initiative carries these risks, some more than others. A prudent growth strategy isn't built on picking a few initiatives and hoping for success, though you wouldn't know that from looking at the growth plans of many major businesses today. Instead, a steady and reliable plan derives from building a portfolio of growth initiatives and managing it with the same care as an investment portfolio.

Manage Portfolio Risk

Markets change, competitors react, customers vary, execution is uncertain. What makes a growth strategy both exciting and frustrating is the range of risks and challenges that must be mastered to achieve success. Despite these inherent uncertainties, few companies today use the best available tool to cope with such risks—portfolio planning. By carefully selecting the best growth tactics, balancing the selections against management goals, and giving due consideration to marketplace and execution constraints, you can achieve double-digit growth within manageable risk tolerances.

The portfolio approach provides a comprehensive framework for managing growth. But it requires constant attention in at least four major areas: It must be adapted to changing market conditions. It must be diversified to reduce risk. It requires a high level of management talent as well as a comprehensive management system. Let's take each in turn.

Meet the Market

Wise investors skew their portfolios toward one sector or another, toward equities or toward bonds, depending on existing market conditions. Managers of growth portfolios should follow suit.

The two key dimensions that affect the balance of a growth portfolio are market growth rates and customer-churn rates. As we saw in Chapter 3, First Data Corporation balanced its growth portfolios differently for its three main divisions because of the varying market conditions each faced. In the money-transfer division, a fast-growing market yielded plenty of growth opportunities simply by concentrating on base retention, share gain, and market positioning. In a slow-growing market, such as the one First Data's card division faced, it was necessary to look for growth opportunities in adjacent markets.

We see the same effect when we compare different companies. Biomet, for example, competes in a steadily growing market for orthopedic implants. It hasn't had to venture far from home base. By contrast, Mohawk's core carpeting business is growing much more slowly and it has ventured into several flooring product adjacencies that put it in competition with other companies.

Rates of customer churn should also influence a growth portfolio's makeup. In a high-churn market, such as mobile telephone service, growth initiatives should be tipped toward base retention and share gain. Nextel, for example, enjoyed a superior growth rate to Sprint PCS simply because it focused on creating superior base retention. Share gain is a great strategy in a churning market because customers are actively looking for a better supplier. In a low-churn market there is little opportunity for organic share gain, and base retention is typically not much of a challenge. As a result, companies in pursuit of double-digit growth seek superior market positioning and adjacent-market penetration. That's what retail banks have done as they try to cross-sell additional products from their new outposts in adjacent markets.

Churn rates also affect the balance between organic growth strategies and a reliance on acquisitions. In general, low-churn businesses can be attractive acquisition candidates for share gain, market positioning, or adjacent-market entry. That's because a stable and assured customer base is so costly and difficult to obtain through organic means. In high-churn markets, acquisitions may yield valuable assets, but assured revenue and customer base are not apt to be among them.

I should note here that acquisition-driven growth has a bad reputation that is often undeserved. Somehow, the investment community has come to see it as less valid than the organic approach, which is viewed as the tough, proper way to grow. Yet as we've seen, there are legitimate roles for an acquisition strategy in market-share gain, market positioning, adjacent growth, and new lines of business. If these purchases can be made using the company's retained capital, they are simply a legitimate alternative to spending the same money on organic growth initiatives.

Diversify

One of the most powerful functions of a portfolio is to reduce risk through diversification. Let's say you want to invest in biotechnology.

By splitting your money among the leaders in the industry, rather than putting it into a single company, you avoid the danger that the one company will falter relative to its peers.

Diversification strategies can be created for each of the four principal growth risks attendant to any growth initiative. For example, assume that your company has analyzed an adjacent market and concluded that it is a highly attractive opportunity for growth and that your core capabilities can be leveraged to achieve a competitive advantage. Your analysis gives you confidence that the demand risks are manageable, but the other risks might still undo your plan. If you develop just one initiative for entering that market, you can be undone by a wily competitor, unexpected implementation problems, or a hitch in your operations. On the other hand, if you develop several complementary growth initiatives for entering the market, your risk of failure is much diminished. You might, for example, look for allies to share one or more aspects of the initiative. At the same time, you might acquire a small competitor as a platform for further growth in the market and also launch your own organic growth initiative in another segment of the same market. If these three growth initiatives are complementary and coordinated, they can accelerate growth within the adjacency and simultaneously lower your competitor, implementation, and operating risks.

This is precisely what Dell Computer has done, pushing ever deeper into the professional-services market. Dell has built an alliance with EMC Corporation to sell their combined expertise in integrating large-capacity data-storage devices. It has also expanded its in-house professional-services capabilities by hiring industry experts and enlarging its own staff. In the middle of all this, in May 2002, the company bought Plural, a two-hundred-person services boutique with special skills in Microsoft systems implementation. In its move into the computer professional-services market, Dell has adopted a variety of growth initiatives to reduce its risk and increase its chances of success.

Although Home Depot will not admit it, the giant retailer has apparently taken dead aim at Sears, developing a multitude of growth initiatives for invading longtime Sears markets. It has decided that the competitive risk is quite manageable and has devised an incursion strategy based on diversified target markets, implementation techniques, and operations.

With the aid of Emerson Electric and Black & Decker, Home Depot has developed rugged, low-cost power tools, going head-to-head with Sears's dominant Craftsman line. The company has also added appliances to its sales mix, using its logistics efficiency to take on another Sears strength. In its latest move, Home Depot has introduced home services, ranging from carpet and siding installation to deck and garage construction, using a network of independent service agents. In short, Home Depot has mounted a diversified attack on Sears's core markets.

Wanted: Management Talent

Despite all the similarities between investment portfolios and growth portfolios, there is one important difference. Once you buy a stock, your risk depends on the skill of distant managers beyond your control. In growth portfolios, however, the outcome depends entirely on the performance of your own company's managers. You have met the masters of your destiny, and they are yourselves.

Consider demand risk. Certainly there are things about market demand that are unknowable—what shoe style or soft-drink taste will be most popular a year or two from now, for example. But the greater part of demand uncertainty is built on what is unknown, what management has failed to learn, not on what is unknowable.

Entrepreneurs understand this only too well. They enter markets based on careful study and planning only to discover a great gap in their knowledge. Sometimes the newfound understanding can be quickly assimilated and the direction changed, but all too often these unknowns beget defeat. And the fault lies not with some elusive mystery of the market, but with management's inability to uncover all the facts.

Competitor risk has the greatest inherent uncertainty; it is usually the least knowable of any of the four types of risk. Customers may be a little flighty and hard to discern, but competitors can be downright indecipherable. In fact, that is their objective. Yet competitor risk cannot hold a candle to implementation risk and operations risk as the real-life reasons for the failure of growth initiatives. That's because they are almost entirely a measure of management capacity.

Precisely because it has such deep management capacities, a company such as Wal-Mart can grow in many varied ways. Its core mass merchandising business is a powerhouse driven by base retention and market share gain. The company has successfully repositioned itself in nine international markets with more than one thousand stores opened since 1991. Combating its Goliath image, it has cleverly begun planting smaller-format Neighborhood Markets all over the U.S. It has also invaded groceries, a major adjacent market that required a new superstore layout for selling food along with everything else. Given so many simultaneous growth initiatives, the risks of implementation, competition, and operations would have overwhelmed the managers of nearly any other company.

To be sure, there are rare instances when the owners of investment portfolios rebel against the managers of growth portfolios. This happens when shareholders and managers turn out to have clashing tolerances for risk.

John Pepper, Procter & Gamble's former CEO, knows well the inhibitions that balky shareholders can cause. In 1997, when Pepper announced his aspiration to double the business by 2004, he evoked a swift and negative reaction from some of the company's largest shareholders. They explained that they had invested in P&G as a steady, reliable earner and not as a growth machine. They felt that Pepper's goal, a growth rate of 14 percent per year, would put steady earnings (and dividends) at risk by forcing the company to engage in chancy acquisitions and product-development investments. The management team knuckled under, lowering the goals to 4 to 6 percent annual growth in revenue and 10 percent growth in profits. That's why the plan to double the business has been pushed out another twenty-five years.

Wanted: A New Management System

Every company has a management system for controlling financial performance. We need a parallel system for managing growth.

In most financial control systems, budgets and reports provide current and actionable information with which to understand, diagnose, and predict financial performance. Routine processes handle financial review and control. Monthly meetings cascade upward within the company, reviewing financial performance against precise, preset targets. The targets are discrete, measurable, and relevant to the people performing the review. Specialists guide the process, but financial responsibility cascades downward throughout the business. Someone is accountable for every budgetary item. A financial control system also has a culture—a system of attitudes, beliefs, and behaviors—that reinforces standards and performance.

A similar management system is needed to plan and control corporate growth. If growth is managed simply as the revenue line item in a financial control system, it will never receive the attention it requires to achieve the best results. Let's consider what such a growth-management system would look like.

The foundation of any management system is accurate, detailed, and timely information. Remember the simple questions in Chapter 1? They revealed whether your organization has the information needed to interpret past growth performance. Even more information and analysis are required to plan for the future.

Suppose your company wants to increase market share at twice the current rate. How much additional value must it provide customers in order to achieve this? How much would the added value cost the company? To what extent would increased revenues offset the cost? The information enabling managers to answer such questions should be as accessible as a monthly cost report or a budget, if growth is to be managed effectively.

In most companies, the line item called revenue has not been sufficiently decomposed and analyzed to allow important growth questions to be answered. External data—such as the rate of base retention among competitors, the responsiveness of customers to value improvements, and the rate of growth of various market segments—are often uncollected. In some cases, even accurate market share information is unavailable to management in a timely and accurate fashion. We have untold detail on the cost side of the business, but revenue and growth information have, for the most part, been sadly neglected.

The first step toward repairing that neglect is to establish a Growth Reconciliation Statement that can attribute changes in revenues and gross profits to particular markets, growth disciplines, and specific initiatives. At a minimum, the statement would set forth gains in revenues and gross profits in each of the core, adjacent, and new markets in which your company competes. It would allow you to easily answer the following questions:

- What is the growth rate of each segment within the market?
- What proportion of our business is in each segment?
- What share of each segment do we control?
- How much was lost to customer defections during the period?
- How much was gained from growth in demand among customers at the start of the period?
- How much was gained from customers new to our business?

A system to manage a growth portfolio requires review, evaluation, and diagnosis processes that can lead to accurate prediction and corrective action. For those processes to work, clear and discrete targets must be set for each growth discipline and translated into smaller and smaller discrete goals as they cascade downward through the organization. Responsibility and authority must be distributed and assigned along with the goals.

A business-unit leader may now be responsible not only for the usual cost targets but for more than a dozen growth targets as well. Line managers and staff members will get specific roles in helping the unit leader to meet those targets.

For any growth-management system to work effectively, you need a culture of reinforcing attitudes and beliefs. If your management team doesn't believe that double-digit growth is vital, it won't happen. And the commitment to growth must pervade the entire organization. Everyone at every level should get a piece of the growth action and feel proud of sharing the company's progress.

When your company has developed a management system for growth that is as robust as its financial control system, it will have left behind forever the days of unpredictable and risky growth. You will be managing growth as it deserves to be managed.

As in the beginning of my book, so at the end, I find myself in the role of pitchman for growth, for which I make no apology. I'm in good company. "Growth is the only evidence of life," wrote John Henry Newman, the great nineteenth-century English writer and Catholic cardinal. Precisely the same rule applies to companies: growth is the only proof of true business success.

I hope that the information and analysis presented here have convinced you that sustainable, double-digit growth is a realistic and attainable business goal. Quite simply, it can be achieved by thoroughly mastering and aggressively pursuing the five disciplines that make up the growth portfolio. The target is visible. The tools are available. The payoff is enormous. The rest is up to you.

Index

215